Bed & Breakfast Cookbook

Also by Pamela Lanier
The Complete Guide to
Bed & Breakfast Inns and Guesthouses
of the United States and Canada
(John Muir Publications)

Bed
&
Breakfast
Cookbook

by Pamela Lanier

Woodchuck Hill Farm
Grafton, Vermont

Running Press
Philadelphia ✦ Pennsylvania

9 8 7 6 5 4 3 2 1
Digit on the right indicates the number of this printing.

Library of Congress Cataloging in Publishing Data:
Lanier, Pamela.
  The bed and breakfast cookbook.
  Includes index.
  1. Cookery. 2. Breakfasts. 3. Brunches. I. Title.
TX652.L247 1985   641.5′3   84–27658

ISBN: 0–89471–329–9 (Paper)

Judy Jacobs, Project Coordinator
Karen Young Joffe, Culinary Editor
Cover design by Toby Schmidt
Cover illustration by Vicki Fox
Typography: Baskerville and Paladium by rci, Philadelphia, PA
and Italian Script by Composing Room, Philadelphia, PA
Printed by Port City Press, Baltimore, MD

This book can be ordered by mail from the publisher.
Please include $1.00 for postage.
But try your bookstore first.
Running Press
Book Publishers
125 South 22nd Street
Philadelphia, Pennsylvania 19103

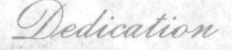

Dedication

This book is dedicated to C. L. Georgie Lanier
and to Corinne Rednour Lanier,
my wonderful parents.

Many thanks to the chefs who took time
to send us their recipes and suggestions, and
special thanks to Ken Luboff, a man with many
talents and lots of good ideas.

Special thanks also to my friends
who helped me with this book, including
Carol McBride, Megan Daane, Elaine Young,
Hodi Hatch, Kitty Locke and Leslie Chan.

Our special thanks to the Bed & Breakfast inns
who provided us with line drawings of their
respective establishments.

Table of Contents

Introduction

*B*ed and breakfast inns (B&Bs) allow the traveller to be immersed in the elegance of an antebellum plantation, to sleep in an historic landmark, to get away from it all on a Colorado ranch or to try houseboating in San Francisco. Whatever the setting, the personal and convivial atmosphere of a B & B provides the chance to make new friends and relax while vacationing. All the little B & B extras that one doesn't expect from an impersonal hotel add up to a special travel experience that is winning over all who travel the B & B route.

Of course, breakfast is an essential ingredient in the B & B experience. This cookbook is a collection of innkeepers' favorite recipes of outstanding regional American cuisine, from Southern biscuits and pecan pie to Northeastern blueberry muffins to Southwestern huevos rancheros. And because brunch, teatime and the cocktail hour are also common culinary customs in America's inns, we include B & B dishes to be served at these times as well. Some will spark the imagination of even the most discriminating gourmet, while others will be perfect for that hectic Sunday morning when you want to do something special but haven't got much time or energy.

Most of the recipes are simple and easy to prepare, but they cover a wide range of cooking styles from a diverse variety of kitchens. Some chefs are precise and detailed in their instructions; others leave much up to the individual cook. To make the preparation of the dishes easier, we have endeavored to standardize the measurements and procedures—without detracting from the unique style of each contributing chef. In addition to the recipes, we have included a short profile of each inn, along with reservation information, to help you with your future travel plans. When you visit each inn, you can taste its specialties for yourself.

Where two recipes from the same inn follow one another, reservation information follows the second recipe. Our charge-card key is as follows: MC equals MasterCard, AE equals American Express, V equals Visa, DC is Diner's Club, CB is Carte Blanche.

Price ranges are based on the rate, per person, for an average double room during the height of the season. Inexpensive is under $35; Moderate is $35 to $55; Expensive is $55 to $85; and over $85 is Very Expensive.

Bon appetit!

Part 1

BREAKFAST

Eiler's Inn
Laguna Beach, California

Breakfast

At the heart of every traveller's dreams is an inn where everything possible is done to please the guests. Thanks to abundant fresh produce and the creativity of their kitchens, America's innkeepers have created some of the most imaginative and delicious dishes ever to grace a breakfast table.

These recipes offer a glimpse of the diversity of America's regional cuisine. The style, of course, varies regionally as well as from inn to inn, but with the recipes on the following pages, you can create these treats over and over again.

The variety is not just in the food, however. There are just as many kinds of breakfasts as there are inns. Luxury establishments pride themselves on exquisite cuisine graciously presented. At the Red Clover Inn in Mendon, Vermont, the innkeeper—who is also the chef—delights his guests with candlelit breakfasts with classical music playing in the background. Country and small town inns often offer very substantial breakfasts with several choices of entrées, freshly baked fruit breads, juices and cereal. The call to breakfast at Captain Jefferd's Inn in Kennebunkport, Maine, is the theme music from *Upstairs/Downstairs*. Guests assemble around the edge of a banquet table flanked by a dozen hand-painted chairs, are personally introduced, and then are served by a white-jacketed waiter.

Other inns provide breakfast at small tables for individual parties, where the food is either served to your exact specifications or is the day's special dish. At Santa Fe's Grant Corner Inn, individual hearty breakfasts consist of separate sideboards: one for beverages, including several kinds of coffees and teas; another for cereals, granola and cornflakes; and the entrée. In addition, a plate of fresh fruit and a basket of sweet rolls and breads are served at your table.

Of course, food is not the only factor that contributes to an enjoyable eating experience. The mood of the meal is also created by the place setting, the china, the tablecloth, the vase of flowers in the center of the table—and the smile on the host or hostess's face.

HOME OF GLORIA BANTZ

Waffles

½ package active dry yeast
1¼ cups warm water
  (100° to 115°,
  approximately)
1½ cups whole wheat flour

¼ cup milk, lukewarm
1½ tablespoons honey
3 tablespoons melted butter
1 teaspoon salt
2 eggs, lightly beaten

The night before serving, dissolve yeast in warm water. Mix in flour and let stand overnight in a warm, draft-free location.

Next morning, heat the waffle iron. Mix together milk, honey and melted butter. Add salt and eggs. Stir into flour/yeast mixture. Cook about five minutes on the waffle iron. Waffles can be reheated in the toaster. Serves 6.

GLORIA BANTZ
82 Vermont Terrace
Tuckahoe, New York
10707
(914) 779-6411

No credit cards
Moderate

Ms. Bantz keeps bees and serves guests honey from her own hives.

MOUNTAIN VIEW INN

Strings of Flats

Stacks of these griddle cakes were consumed in great quantity in the old lumbering camps, where they were known as flannel cakes (for the flannel shirts worn by lumberjacks) and as strings of flats (as in flatcars, the railroad cars that carried the lumber to market).

2 egg whites
1 cup all-purpose flour
1 tablespoon baking
  powder
½ teaspoon salt

2 tablespoons sugar
2 egg yolks
1 cup milk
2 tablespoons hot bacon
  grease

Beat egg whites until stiff. Sift together flour, baking powder, salt and sugar. Mix yolks and milk together and stir quickly into dry ingredients. Gently fold in beaten egg whites. After mixture is relatively smooth, fold in bacon grease. Cook pancakes on a hot grill. Serve with home-cured bacon, butter and lots of Vermont maple syrup. Serves 2 to 4, depending on appetites.

MOUNTAIN VIEW INN
Route 17, RFD Box 69
Waitsfield, Vermont
05673
(802) 496-2426

No credit cards
Moderate

The antique-filled Mountain View Inn has seven guestrooms. Homecooked country meals are served around a large harvest table.

Bell Creek Sourdough Waffles

1 cup whole wheat flour,
  unsifted
1 cup unsifted unbleached
  all-purpose flour
½ cup Sourdough Starter

2 cups buttermilk
2 eggs, beaten
½ cup milk
½ cup butter, melted
cooking oil

In a bowl, combine wheat flour, unbleached flour, Sourdough Starter and buttermilk. (Sourdough Starter packets are available by mail from Williams-Sonoma, 576 Sutter Street, San Francisco, CA 94102.) Beat until blended. Cover and let stand at room temperature 45 minutes or preferably overnight. (In warm weather, put in refrigerator overnight.)

Beat together eggs, milk and melted butter. Add to flour mixture and stir until blended. Preheat electric waffle iron, brush grids with oil, spoon proper amount into iron and bake. When lightly browned, serve with syrup or apple butter (see following recipe) and, if desired, butter. Makes about 4 large waffles. These waffles freeze well. Reheat frozen waffles in toaster. Serves 4.

Our Own Apple Butter

1 cup thick applesauce
½ cup sugar

½ teaspoon cinnamon
⅛ teaspoon cloves

Combine all ingredients and cook slowly until mixture attains the desired thickness. If applesauce is made of very bland apples, add up to a tablespoon of lemon juice to taste.

Yields 1½ cups.

BELL CREEK B & B
3220 Silverado Trail
St. Helena, California
94574
(707) 257-0557

No credit cards
Moderate

Hidden in a walnut orchard in the heart of the Napa Valley wine country, the two-guestroom Bell Creek B & B is homey, simple, and has its own swimming pool.

Garland's Oak Creek Lodge
Sedona, Arizona

Pancakes à la Millbrook

2 cups all-purpose flour
1 teaspoon salt
2 tablespoons sugar
4 teaspoons baking powder
2 eggs, lightly beaten

2½ cups milk
2 tablespoons butter,
  melted
1 pint strawberries or
  raspberries (optional)

Mix flour, salt, sugar and baking powder in a large bowl. In another bowl, whisk eggs and milk together with a wire whisk. Stir in butter. Pour wet ingredients (eggs, milk, and butter mixture) over dry ingredients (flour, salt, sugar and baking powder) and mix with a wooden spoon until just blended. The batter should be lumpy. Pour ¼ cup batter per pancake onto a hot griddle. (For blueberry or strawberry pancakes, sprinkle fresh blueberries or sliced fresh strawberries on the pancakes as soon as you pour the batter onto griddle.) Cook until cakes are full of air bubbles on top and lightly browned on underside. Flip over to brown the other side. Serves 6.

MILLBROOK INN
RFD Box 62, Route 17
Waitsfield, Vermont
05673
(802) 496-2405

MC/V
Expensive

Guests can relax in this charming six-room country inn's unhurried atmosphere and revel in its candlelit dinners.

Banana Buttermilk Buckwheat Pancakes

1 cup all-purpose flour
½ cup whole wheat flour
½ cup buckwheat flour
2 tablespoons sugar
1 teaspoon salt
1 teaspoon baking soda
4 teaspoons baking powder

2 eggs, lightly beaten
4 tablespoons butter,
  melted
1½ cups buttermilk
½ cup milk
2 ripe bananas, mashed

In a large bowl, combine all-purpose flour, whole wheat flour, buckwheat flour, sugar, salt, baking soda and baking powder. In another bowl, combine remaining ingredients. Add liquid mixture to the dry ingredients, stirring well. Drop by ⅓ cupfuls onto a 350° griddle. Serves 4 to 6.

TEN INVERNESS WAY
10 Inverness Way
Inverness, California
94937
(415) 669-1648

No credit cards
Moderate

This five-room inn is located an hour or so north of San Francisco and not far from the scenic beauty of Point Reyes National Seashore.

S T O N E H U R S T   M A N O R

Cornmeal and Bacon Pancakes

⅓ cup yellow cornmeal
1 cup all-purpose flour
1 teaspoon salt
2 teaspoons baking powder
1 egg

1¼ cup milk
1 tablespoon bacon fat,
  melted
2 strips bacon, cooked and
  crumbled

Mix together cornmeal, flour, salt and baking powder. In a separate bowl, beat the egg, add milk and then bacon fat. Stir this mixture slowly into the dry ingredients, mixing well. The batter should be fairly thin; add more milk if necessary. Finally mix in crumbled bacon. Cook pancakes in a skillet or on a griddle. Serve with butter and maple syrup. Serves 4.

STONEHURST INN
P.O. Box 1900
Conway, New Hampshire
03860
(603) 356-3113

MC/V/AE
Moderate to very
expensive

The elegance of another era pervades this beautiful 24-room English-style country inn with rooms in every price range. The Stonehurst Inn is situated on 33 pine-forested acres.

The Headlands Inn
Mendocino, California

HERSEY HOUSE

Gingerbread Pancakes

This recipe comes from Dee Maaske, an actress who has performed with the Ashland Shakespeare Festival.

2½ cups all-purpose flour
5 teaspoons baking powder
1½ teaspoons salt
1 teaspoon baking soda
1 teaspoon cinnamon
½ teaspoon ginger

¼ cup molasses
2 cups milk
2 eggs, lightly beaten
6 tablespoons butter,
  melted
1 cup raisins

HERSEY HOUSE
451 North Main Street
Ashland, Oregon
97520
(503) 482-4563

No credit cards
Expensive

This four-room Victorian farmhouse is located in the center of Ashland, site of the renowned annual Shakespeare Festival.

Sift together flour, baking powder, salt, soda and spices. Combine molasses and milk and add eggs, stirring to blend. Stir in melted butter. Add molasses mixture to dry ingredients. Stir only until moistened. Mix in raisins. Cook on a hot griddle, using ¼ cup batter for each pancake. Serves 8.

THE MONTE CRISTO

Gooseberry Pancakes

1 cup whole wheat pastry
  flour
½ cup buckwheat flour
½ cup unbleached all-
  purpose flour
3 teaspoons baking
  powder
1 teaspoon salt

1 tablespoon brown sugar
  or honey
3 eggs, lightly beaten
2 cups milk
1 stick (4 ounces) butter,
  melted
1 cup gooseberries,
  cooked or canned

THE MONTE CRISTO
600 Presidio Avenue
San Francisco, California
94115
(415) 931-1875

MC/V/AE
Moderate to
very expensive

Located in San Francisco's exclusive Presidio Heights district, this inn is within walking distance of restored Victorian shops, restaurants and antique dealers.

Sift flours with baking powder, salt and sugar (not honey). Beat together eggs, milk and melted butter. If using honey, add it to the milk and eggs mixture. Combine liquids with dry ingredients, stirring until just barely mixed. Fold in gooseberries. Cook on a hot griddle or in a greased frying pan. Serve with maple syrup and butter. Serves 6.

HARBOR HOUSE BY THE SEA

Souffléed Apple Pancakes

¼ cup (½ stick) unsalted
  butter
2 tart apples, peeled, cored
  and thickly sliced
¾ cups half-and-half
½ cup all-purpose flour
¼ teaspoon salt
3 egg yolks, lightly beaten

2 tablespoons unsalted
  butter, melted and
  cooled to room
  temperature
3 egg whites
pinch of cream of tartar
pinch of salt
1 tablespoon sugar
1 tablespoon butter

Preheat broiler.

In a stainless steel sauté pan or enameled skillet, melt the butter and sauté the apple slices, turning them carefully while cooking so they do not break. Cook until tender (about 6 minutes).

In a bowl, combine half-and-half, flour, ¼ teaspoon salt, egg yolks (one at a time) and the melted butter. In another bowl, beat the egg whites with cream of tartar and salt until they hold soft peaks. Add the sugar and continue beating until the whites hold stiff peaks. Stir ¼ of the whites into the batter to lighten it, then gently fold in the remaining whites. Melt 1 tablespoon butter in a flameproof 10″ skillet (with an 8″ bottom) over moderate heat. When it is hot, add half of the batter, spreading it evenly with a spatula. Cook the pancake for 3 minutes. Arrange half of the apple slices decoratively over the pancake, and put the pancake under the broiler, 4″ from the source of heat, for 2 to 3 minutes or until puffed and golden brown. Slide the pancake onto a serving plate and keep warm. Make another pancake in the same manner with the remaining batter and apple slices. Serve the pancakes with maple syrup. Serves 4 as a breakfast dish or 8 (cut pancakes into wedges) as a dessert.

HARBOR HOUSE
BY THE SEA
5600 South Highway #1
P.O. Box 369
Elk, California
95432
(707) 877-3203

No credit cards
Moderate

In the tiny Mendocino town of Elk, the Harbor House by the Sea has five rooms, four cottages and its own private beach.

GRANT CORNER INN

Dutch Babies

¼ cup butter
3 eggs
¾ cup milk
¾ cup all-purpose flour

banana topping (see
  following recipe)
2 cups lightly sweetened
  whipped cream

Preheat oven to 425°.

Put butter in a large cast-iron skillet and put skillet in hot oven. While butter is melting, beat eggs with electric mixer set at high speed for one minute. Whisk in milk alternately with flour, just until blended (may be slightly lumpy). Remove hot skillet from oven and pour batter onto melted butter. Bake 20 to 25 minutes or until brown and puffy. Dust with powdered sugar and serve immediately with banana topping and lightly sweetened whipped cream. Serves 4.

BANANA TOPPING
3 ripe bananas
3 tablespoons lemon juice
2 teaspoons cinnamon

pinch of nutmeg
banana brandy

Chop bananas, add lemon juice, cinnamon and nutmeg. Blend in banana brandy to taste.

GRANT CORNER INN
122 Grant Avenue
Santa Fe, New Mexico
87501
(505) 983-6678

MC/V
Expensive

This elegant colonial home is set in one of America's most charming western towns.

GRANE'S FAIRHAVEN INN

Orange Tipsy French Toast

6 eggs, lightly beaten
2 tablespoons light cream
pinch of salt
2 tablespoons Triple Sec
  liqueur
1 tablespoon maple syrup

1 teaspoon grated orange
  rind
½ teaspoon grated
  nutmeg
1 baguette of French
  bread, thinly sliced

In a bowl, mix together all ingredients except bread slices. Soak bread in liquid mixture until all has been absorbed, turning the slices once. Cook on a hot griddle in cooking oil, turning to brown both sides. Serve with syrup and butter. Serves 6.

GRANE'S FAIRHAVEN INN
North Bath Road
Bath, Maine
04530
(207) 443-4391

No credit cards
Moderate

Using Grane's Fairhaven Inn as a base, guests can participate in a wide variety of outdoor activities, including hiking, ocean swimming, golfing, boating, fishing, skiing and snowshoeing.

Swag Granola Cereal

1½ cups rolled oats
¼ cup sesame seeds
½ cup sunflower seeds
½ cup shredded
   unsweetened coconut
½ cup wheat germ
¼ cup bran

½ cup almonds
¼ cup oil
¼ cup honey
½ teaspoon vanilla extract
½ teaspoon almond extract
raisins or other dried fruit,
   as desired

Preheat oven to 300°.

Tumble together oats, sesame seeds, sunflower seeds, coconut, wheat germ, bran and almonds in a big bowl. Heat oil and honey together in saucepan until thin and fairly hot. Remove from heat and stir in vanilla and almond extracts. Pour over dry ingredients and stir to coat evenly. Spread in single layers on jelly roll pans and toast in oven, stirring from time to time, until evenly browned. Remove from oven and allow to cool thoroughly. Stir in raisins or other dried fruit. Serves 8 to 10. Recipe can be doubled and stored in tightly-covered containers.

THE SWAG
Route 2, P.O. Box 280-A
Waynesville, North Carolina
28786

MC/V
Very expensive

A rustic hewn-log lodge located on a breath-taking mountaintop clearing, The Swag serves meals that are as impressive as the surroundings.

Golden Granola

1½ cups Quaker
   Old-Fashioned Oats
½ cup chopped nuts, any
   kind
½ cup shredded coconut

½ teaspoon cinnamon
⅛ cup butter, melted
⅛ cup honey
½ teaspoon vanilla
½ cup raisins or dried fruit

Preheat oven to 350°.

Mix oats, nuts, coconut and cinnamon in an ungreased baking dish. (To increase crispiness, one cup of cornflakes can be substituted for one cup of oats.) Combine melted butter, honey and vanilla. Pour over dry ingredients and mix. Bake granola for 30 to 40 minutes, stirring every 5 to 10 minutes to prevent burning. When evenly golden-colored, remove and, while cooling, add raisins or fruit. Serves 12. Recipe can be doubled and stored in tightly-covered containers.

HUMPHREY HUGHES
HOUSE
29 Ocean Street
Cape May, New Jersey
08204
(609) 884-4428

MC/V/AE
Expensive

A restored Victorian home in the historic seaside town of Cape May, the Humphrey Hughes House serves a special Sunday breakfast.

L I N D E N

Lil's Eggs from Linden

4 squirts Pam™ vegetable
  cooking spray
4 eggs

4 teaspoons half-and-half
2 tablespoons grated
  cheese

Preheat oven to 450°. Spray 4 muffin tins with Pam™.

Drop a raw egg into each tin. Cover each egg with a tea-spoon of half-and-half. Sprinkle grated cheese over the top. Bake for 10 minutes. Gently remove eggs from tin and place on plates. Serves 4.

Lil's Grits from Linden

1 quart water
½ cup regular grits
1 cube beef bouillon

½ stick (4 tablespoons)
  butter
salt to taste

In a saucepan, bring the water to a boil. Stir in the grits, bouillon cube and butter. Cook for 15 to 20 minutes, stirring frequently. Consistency should be slightly thick, but not soupy. Add salt to taste. Serves 4.

LINDEN
1 Linden Place
Natchez, Mississippi
39120
(601) 445-5472

No credit cards
Expensive

An antebellum Southern mansion with a doorway used in the filming of *Gone With the Wind*, the Linden is noted for its outstanding collection of federal-period antique furniture and has been awarded Four Dia-monds by Mobil.

Mountain View Inn
Waitsfield, Vermont

Hill Farm Inn French Toast

4 eggs
1 cup milk
4 teaspoons sugar
¼ teaspoon salt

½ teaspoon vanilla
8 slices homemade white
 bread, cut thickly

In a 13" by 9" baking dish, beat eggs, milk, sugar, salt and vanilla until fluffy. Add bread to dish, turning after it has soaked up about half of the mixture. When the bread is thoroughly soaked, use a pancake turner to transfer it to a hot buttered griddle (370°). Cook about 4 minutes on each side, or until golden brown. Serve with Vermont maple syrup. Serves 4 to 8.

HILL FARM INN
R.R. 2, Box 2015
Arlington, Vermont
05250
(802) 375-2269

MC/V
Moderate

Hiking, fishing and full country breakfasts are just a few of the pleasures awaiting guests at this seven-room, three-cabin establishment, which has been in operation for more than 75 years.

Super-Duper French Toast

6 eggs
⅔ cup orange juice
⅓ cup Grand Marnier
⅓ cup milk
3 tablespoons sugar
¼ teaspoon vanilla
¼ teaspoon salt

finely grated peel of one
 orange
eight ¾" thick slices
 French bread
3 to 4 tablespoons butter
4 tablespoons powdered
 sugar

The night before, beat eggs in large bowl. Add orange juice, Grand Marnier, milk, sugar, vanilla, salt, and orange peel and mix well. Dip bread into mixture, turning to coat all surfaces. Transfer bread to baking dish in a single layer. Pour any remaining egg mixture over top. Cover and refrigerate overnight, turning occasionally, until liquid is absorbed into bread.

In the morning, melt butter in large skillet over medium-high heat. Add bread slices in batches and cook until browned (about eight minutes). Turn and continue cooking another eight minutes, until brown. Cut bread diagonally. Arrange on platter and sprinkle with powdered sugar. Serve immediately with butter and maple syrup. Serves 4.

SUGAR TREE LODGE
Highway 56
Vesuvius, Virginia
24483
(703) 377-2197

MC/V
Expensive

Constructed from 19th-century log cabins, the Sugar Tree Lodge is located on the edge of the Blue Ridge Mountains in an area popular for hunting, fishing, swimming, horseback riding and hiking.

Smith House Banana Fritters

cooking oil
2⅓ cups all-purpose flour
½ teaspoon baking
   powder
½ teaspoon baking soda
½ teaspoon salt

2 eggs
½ cup sugar
two 13-ounce cans
   evaporated milk
12 bananas, peeled and
   quartered

Fill deep fryer with oil 4 to 5 inches deep and preheat oil to 375°.

Sift flour, baking powder, baking soda and salt together. In a separate bowl, beat together eggs and sugar. To egg mixture add milk alternately with sifted dry ingredients. Beat lightly after each addition to form a thin batter. Dip bananas into the batter and then drop them into hot oil. Fry, turning occasionally, until golden brown. Serves 10 to 12.

This batter can also be used for apple fritters: add ½ teaspoon cinnamon and ½ teaspoon nutmeg to batter and substitute peeled apple slices for banana quarters.

THE SMITH HOUSE
202 Chestatee Street, S.W.
Dahlonega, Georgia
30533
(404) 864-3566

MC/V/AE
Inexpensive

Northern Georgia's Smith House offers Southern hospitality and all-you-can-eat home cooking.

The Gosby House Inn
Pacific Grove, California

The 1883 Fleming Jones Homestead
Placerville, California

DAIRY HOLLOW HOUSE

Apple-Brie Cheese Omelette

½ apple, peeled, cored
  and thinly sliced
2½ tablespoons butter
2 eggs, room temperature

2 teaspoons cream or milk
dash of salt and pepper
2 tablespoons diced Brie
  cheese

Sauté apples in one tablespoon butter in a 5" or 6" omelette pan. Beat together eggs, cream or milk, and salt and pepper until blended but not frothy. Melt remaining butter in omelette pan over high heat until foam begins to recede (but before beginning to color). Pour in egg mixture and prepare omelette, beating to lighten but still allowing it to set on bottom. Fill with sautéed apples and cheese cubes. Fold or roll and slide out of pan onto a heated plate. Serves one.

DAIRY HOLLOW
HOUSE
Rt. 2, Box 1
Eureka Springs, Arkansas
72632
(501) 253-7444

MC/V/AE
Expensive

The Dairy Hollow House is a transformed Ozarks farmhouse filled with folk art and flowers in every room. Its restaurant serves "Noveau (*sic*) Zarks," country cuisine with a French accent.

Fluffy Two-Cheese Omelette

2 tablespoons butter
5 eggs
¼ cup half-and-half or
  milk
pepper to taste
2 tablespoons finely
  chopped chives or
  scallion tops

½ cup grated Tillamook
  cheddar cheese
½ cup grated Turumna
  cheese, or any semi-
  soft, rich white cheese

Preheat oven to 350°.

Heat butter in a heavy skillet. Beat eggs and half-and-half with an electric beater until extremely frothy. Immediately pour into skillet. Sprinkle with pepper and chives. Evenly distribute the 2 cheeses over the top. Cook, tightly covered, about 8 to 10 minutes, or until firm on top. With a spatula, cut the omelette into quarters. Turn 2 quarters over and onto remaining quarters to make 2 separate portions. Serves 2.

Orange Soufflé Omelette

2 tablespoons butter
5 eggs, separated
dash of cream of tartar
1 tablespoon sugar
2 tablespoons all-purpose
  flour
½ teaspoon baking
  powder

½ teaspoon dried orange
  peel or lemon peel
½ cup freshly squeezed and
  strained orange juice
1 cup sour cream
1 cup whole berry
  cranberry sauce
garnish of orange slices

Preheat oven to 350°.

Blend sour cream with cranberry sauce and set aside.

Melt the butter in a heavy cast-iron skillet. Beat egg whites with cream of tartar and sugar until stiff. Blend the flour, baking powder and orange peel in a bowl. Stir in orange juice and egg yolks and beat until frothy. Gently fold in beaten egg whites. Spread this mixture into the melted butter in the heated skillet. Cook, tightly covered, for about 8 minutes or until just firm. Cut into quarters. Turn each quarter carefully over in place, and cook another 5 minutes. Serve with cranberry-sour cream topping, either between the quarters or on the side. Garnish with orange slices. Serves 2.

ELK COVE INN
P.O. Box 367
Elk, California
95432
(707) 877-3321

No credit cards
Moderate to expensive

Hugging the northern Mendocino coastline, the nine-room Elk Cove Inn is an old-fashioned country establishment serving German and French cuisine.

V E N T A N A

Eggs Mousseline

Eggs Mousseline is Ventana's sous-chef Peter Charles's favorite egg dish.

6 brioche rolls
6 tablespoons shaved,
* smoked salmon*
6 poached eggs
1 cup hollandaise sauce,
* room temperature*

1 cup heavy cream,
* whipped*
½ cup chopped fresh dill,
* or to taste*

Re-warm brioches. Remove the tops and some of the soft center. Stuff each roll with a tablespoon of shaved smoked salmon and a poached egg. Prepare the mousseline sauce by folding together equal amounts of hollandaise and whipped cream. Fold in dill. Consistency will continue to resemble that of hollandaise sauce. Ladle sauce over the poached eggs in brioches.

Chef Charles suggests serving a sautéed tomato and spinach mixture on the side: He sautés tomato slices quickly on a clean griddle top and serves three per person. He prepares the spinach by melting clarified butter in a sauté pan, throwing in a pinch of minced garlic, and adding one handful per person of washed whole spinach leaves. Spinach is cooked just long enough to wilt. Serves 6.

VENTANA INN
Highway 1
Big Sur, California
93920
(408) 624-4812

All major credit cards
Very expensive

The dramatic California coastline is the setting for this elegant inn and its Mobil four-star restaurant.

The Gray Whale
Fort Bragg, California

Eggs at Mayhurst

4 hard-boiled eggs
2 eggs, beaten lightly
¼ cup cream
pinch of salt
⅛ teaspoon nutmeg
1 tablespoon fresh lemon
   juice

1 tablespoon butter
2 to 4 English muffin
   halves
2 to 4 slices Virginia
   country ham

Chop hard-boiled eggs, and set aside. Put beaten eggs, cream, salt, nutmeg and lemon juice in top of double boiler and cook until thick, whisking while cooking. This will take only a few minutes. Do not overcook. Remove from stove, stir in butter until it melts, then stir in chopped eggs. Serve over English muffins topped with Virginia country ham. Serves 2 to 4, depending on appetites.

MAYHURST B & B
P.O. Box 707
Orange, Virginia
22960
(703) 672-5597

MC/V
Moderate

This 36-acre Virginia country estate offers visitors lush rolling pastureland and a fishing pond.

L'Omelette Homard Forestier
(Omelette with Lobster and Mushrooms)

butter
4 ounces sliced
   mushrooms
salt and pepper, to taste
¼ cup good port
¼ cup heavy cream

1 fresh lobster tail,
   poached, shelled and
   diced (approximately 1
   cup)
1 ounce clarified butter
2 eggs, lightly beaten
freshly grated Parmesan
   cheese

Sauté mushrooms in butter. Season with salt and pepper. Stir in port and cream. Reduce by half. Add lobster meat and simmer just until the meat is warmed. To a seasoned omelette pan, add clarified butter. Heat the pan, and add the eggs. Stir briskly with a fork to lighten the omelette as it cooks. Add the warmed lobster mixture to the center of the omelette. Fold the omelette over the mixture, slide onto a serving plate and sprinkle with Parmesan cheese. Serve immediately. Serves 2.

EDSON HILL MANOR
R.F.D. 1
Stowe, Vermont
05672
(802) 253-7371

MC/V
Expensive

Cross-country skiing, horseback riding, swimming, hiking and barbecues await visitors to this secluded 400-acre country estate.

*Seafair Inn
Ogunquit, Maine*

LA POSADA DE CHIMAYO

Sofia Trujillo's Red Chili

½ pound diced pork
2 cups water
3 garlic cloves
2 tablespoons fat
2 tablespoons all-purpose
   flour

1 heaping tablespoon
   ground red chili
salt to taste

Bring diced pork, water and garlic to a boil. Lower heat and simmer for about ½ hour, until a nice broth forms. Strain, reserving separately both meat and broth. Melt fat over medium heat. Add flour and cook, stirring, for one minute. Add ground red chili to flour mixture and cook one more minute, stirring constantly. Do not let burn! To the flour-chili mixture add pork broth gradually, stirring constantly; then add the meat. Simmer for 10 to 15 minutes on low heat, stirring occasionally. Salt to taste. Red chili should be the consistency of a thin gravy. Serve over fried eggs with sausage and fried potatoes. Enough for 4 toppings.

LA POSADA DE
CHIMAYO
Box 463
Chimayo, New Mexico
87522
(505) 351-4605

No credit cards
Moderate

Guests in this adobe inn experience the traditional lifestyle and beauty of northern New Mexico, as well as a sampling of its spicy cuisine.

A R D E N   H A L L

Breakfast Casserole

6 slices bread, cubed
1 pound regular or hot
   sausage, cooked, crum-
   bled and drained of fat
1 cup grated cheddar
   cheese

6 eggs, lightly beaten
2 cups milk
1 teaspoon salt
1 teaspoon dry mustard

The night before, layer bread, sausage and grated cheese in a buttered baking dish. Combine eggs, milk, salt and dry mustard, and pour over the ingredients in the baking dish. Refrigerate overnight. In the morning, bake for 45 minutes at 350°. Serves 6.

ARDEN HALL
1052 Arden Drive, S.W.
Marietta, Georgia
30060
(404) 422-0780

No credit cards
Expensive

The small, century-old Arden Hall, located 18 miles from Atlanta, specializes in personalized attention and elegant breakfasts. No smoking is allowed.

T H E   R E D S T O N E   I N N

Huevos Redstone

½ onion, diced
1 stalk celery, diced
½ green pepper, diced
1½ tablespoons paprika
1½ tablespoons chili
   powder
½ teaspoon cumin
½ teaspoon black pepper
½ teaspoon salt
½ teaspoon garlic, minced
½ teaspoon oregano

½ teaspoon Cayenne
   pepper
½ tablespoon chicken base
1 tomato, diced
1 quart water
1 tablespoon cornstarch
8 eggs
8 corn tortillas
2 cups grated cheddar
   cheese
1 cup sour cream

In a saucepan, sauté onion, celery and green pepper until onions are translucent. Stir in the seasonings, chicken base and diced tomato. Add 3 cups water, bring to a boil and simmer for 20 to 30 minutes. Mix cornstarch with remaining cup of water, add to pan and simmer for another 10 minutes. (This sauce is also great for topping chili rellenos or burritos or as a dip with corn chips.)

Fry eggs. Heat corn tortillas until tender. On an oven-proof serving plate, place 2 tablespoons sauce and cover with a tortilla. Top tortillas with eggs and smother with sauce. Top with grated cheese and put under broiler until cheese is melted. Top with sour cream and serve. Serves 8.

THE REDSTONE INN
0082 Redstone Boulevard
Redstone, Colorado
81623
(303) 963-2526

MC/V/AE
Moderate

The historic Redstone Inn was built in 1902 to house miners in a unique village created by a coal baron to prove his theory that people who live in pleasant surroundings are more productive. Today the 35-room inn offers such activities as horseback riding and skiing.

THE UNION HOTEL

Sausage

4 pounds freshly ground
  pork
¾ tablespoon salt
½ tablespoon freshly
  ground pepper
¾ tablespoon powdered
  sage

¾ tablespoon fresh
  ground Cayenne
  pepper
⅛ cup finely chopped
  garlic

Mix all ingredients together thoroughly with your hands and form into 3-inch patties. Cook in a skillet until nicely browned. Serves 20.

Cream Biscuits

2 tablespoons baking
  powder
4 cups all-purpose flour
1 teaspoon salt

¼ pound good quality
  butter (salted, not
  sweet)
1 pint plus 1 tablespoon
  heavy cream

Preheat oven to 400° (or 425° if your oven is slow). Butter a baking sheet and set aside.

Stir together the first 3 ingredients. Cut the butter in coarsely. Add the cream gradually. Knead briefly—just long enough to make a stiff dough. Do not overwork. Roll out to ½" thickness. Cut into squares of desired size. (Cut-dough biscuits hold for 6 hours in the refrigerator. Do not freeze.) Bake 18 minutes, or until puffed and golden in color. Serve immediately. Makes 20 biscuits.

THE UNION HOTEL
401 First Street
Benicia, California
94510
(707) 746-0100

All major credit cards
Expensive

Located in an artists' colony not far from San Francisco, The Union Hotel's 12 individually-decorated rooms will delight lovers of Americana, and all will enjoy the hotel's traditional American cuisine.

The Captain Whidbey Inn
Coupeville, Washington

THE RUPLEY HOUSE INN

German Coffee Cake

2 cups all-purpose flour
2 cups brown sugar
½ cup butter, chilled
1 egg, lightly beaten
1 cup sour milk or
  buttermilk

1 teaspoon baking soda
1 teaspoon vanilla
cinnamon

Preheat oven to 375°. Butter a square baking pan.

In bowl combine flour, brown sugar and butter, working the butter in until it resembles a coarse meal. Set aside one cup of this mixture for topping. To remainder add beaten egg, sour milk, baking soda and vanilla. Stir to blend. Pour into pan. Crumble topping over batter. Sprinkle a little cinnamon over all. Bake 40 minutes. Serves 8.

THE RUPLEY HOUSE
INN
Placerville, California
95667
(916) 626-0630

No credit cards
Moderate to expensive

This 50-acre ranch set in the middle of California's gold rush country invites guests to pan for gold, pet the champion quarter horses, and dine on blue-ribbon baked goods.

THE KENWOOD INN

Pineapple Bread

3 cups sifted all-purpose
  flour
4½ teaspoons baking
  powder
1½ teaspoons salt
½ cup sugar

1 egg, lightly beaten
1½ cups milk
4 tablespoons melted
  butter
1 small can crushed
  pineapple, well drained

Preheat oven to 350°. Butter a 9½" by 5½" loaf pan.

Sift together flour, baking powder, salt and sugar. Combine egg, milk and melted butter, then add drained pineapple. Pour into flour mixture and stir just enough to moisten dry ingredients—do not beat. Turn into loaf pan and bake 50 to 55 minutes, or until tests done. Makes one loaf or 8 servings (16 slices).

THE KENWOOD INN
38 Marine Street
St. Augustine, Florida
32084
(904) 824-2116

MC/V
Moderate

The 15-room, 19th-century Kenwood Inn is located just minutes from the beach in the heart of the oldest city in the United States.

Hotel Strasburg's Fried Tomatoes

3 medium tomatoes, firm
   and not quite ripe
2 cups all-purpose flour
2 teaspoons, more or less,
   garlic powder
1 teaspoon ground cumin
   seed

salt and pepper
1 egg
¾ cup milk
butter

Slice tomatoes into slices ¼″ to ⅜″ wide. Combine flour with seasonings in a shallow bowl. In a separate dish, beat egg, add milk and stir to blend. Dip tomato slices in seasoned flour. Shake off excess flour and dip in egg/milk wash. Dip tomatoes one more time in flour mixture. Allow slices to stand for 10 minutes or more. Sauté in butter for about 2 minutes on each side, or until golden brown. Serves 4 to 6.

Serve with either poached or sunny-side-up eggs, country sausage and whole hominy for a breakfast that will carry you through the day.

HOTEL STRASBURG
201 Holliday Street
Strasburg, Virginia
22657
(703) 465-9191

MC/V/AE/CB/DC
Moderate

Built originally in the 1890s as a private hospital, the Hotel Strasburg has 18 antique-appointed rooms.

Miner's Breakfast

4 large russet potatoes,
   boiled, peeled and
   cubed
9 pieces bacon, fried crisp
   and crumbled
4 tablespoons butter

½ bell pepper, chopped
minced garlic to taste
salt and pepper
8 eggs, lightly beaten
1 cup grated cheddar
   cheese

Preheat oven to 350°.

Melt butter in a skillet, add potato cubes and bell pepper and brown slightly. Add garlic to potatoes. Add salt and pepper to taste. Pour eggs over potatoes and cook until eggs form soft curds, stirring constantly. Mix in crumbled bacon. Sprinkle grated cheese over the top. Place skillet in oven or under broiler until cheese is melted. Serves 6.

THE OLD MINER'S
LODGE
P.O. Box 2639
Park City, Utah
84060
(801) 645-8068

MC/V
Moderate to expensive

In the heart of a favorite recreation and ski area not far from Salt Lake City, the Old Miner's Lodge preserves the spirit of the days when the Lodge was built to house those seeking their fortunes in silver.

The Hanford House
Sutter Creek, California

WEST MOUNTAIN INN

Ooey Gooey

4 large slices of bread
4 tablespoons mayonnaise
8 eggs, fried

2 cups grated Vermont
   cheddar cheese
1 teaspoon paprika

Spread slices of bread with mayonnaise. Top each slice with 2 fried eggs and grated Vermont cheddar cheese. Melt under a broiler. Lightly sprinkle paprika on melted cheese to enhance flavor and add color. Serves 4.

WEST MOUNTAIN INN
Off Route 313
Arlington, Vermont
05250
(802) 375-6516

MC/V/AE
Moderate

There's plenty to do around the West Mountain Inn: bicycling on beautiful country roads; swimming, fishing, canoeing and tubing on the Battenkill River; and hiking or wilderness cross-country skiing on woodland trails.

THE CAPTAIN LORD MANSION

Rick's Soft-Boiled Eggs

Take eggs cold from the refrigerator and poke each with a pin to make small holes in the large ends. Place eggs in boiling water and boil for five minutes. (It is best to use a timer for this!) Remove the eggs and run them under cold water to stop the cooking action. Place each egg in an egg cup and cut off the tops with an egg topper.

Bev's Cranberry Bread

5 cups all-purpose flour	2 eggs
2½ cups sugar	2 cups fresh orange juice
1 teaspoon baking soda	8 tablespoons (1 stick)
3 teaspoons baking	butter, melted
powder	1 cup water
2 teaspoons salt	2 cups cranberries

Preheat oven to 325°. Grease 3 loaf pans and dust with flour.

Sift together flour, sugar, baking soda, baking powder and salt. In a large measuring cup, combine eggs, orange juice, melted butter and water. Make a well in the center of the dry ingredients. Using a whisk or large spoon, stir wet ingredients into well of dry ingredients until all is combined. Fold in cranberries and pour batter into the prepared loaf tins. Bake for one hour, or until bread tests done. Makes 3 loaves.

THE CAPTAIN LORD MANSION
P.O. Box 527
Kennebunkport, Maine 04046
(207) 967-3141

No credit cards
Expensive

This 16-room mansion considers itself "an intimate Maine coast inn" and keeps in touch with former guests through an annual newsletter.

*The Briggs House
Sacramento, California*

HAWTHORNE INN

Brown Breakfast Bread

HAWTHORNE INN
462 Lexington Road
Concord, Massachusetts
01742
(617) 369-5610

No credit cards
Expensive

Located on land that once belonged to Ralph Waldo Emerson, the Alcotts and Nathaniel Hawthorne, the inn is filled with antique furnishings, handmade quilts and sculpture created by the innkeeper.

¾ cup honey
¾ cup molasses
3½ cups all-purpose flour
2 teaspoons baking soda
2 teaspoons ginger
2 teaspoons cinnamon
2 teaspoons allspice
dash of salt
2 cups milk
1 cup raisins
2 tablespoons orange marmalade

Preheat oven to 350°. Butter a large baking dish.

Beat together honey and molasses. Stir in remaining ingredients until just blended. Bake for 1¼ hours, or until done.

EL PARADERO

Huevos Rancheros por Gringos

1 large onion, chopped
1 clove garlic, minced
1 tablespoon oil
one 4-ounce can chopped green chilies or 3 large fresh chilies, skinned and chopped
one 32-ounce can stewed tomatoes
one 8-ounce can tomato sauce
one 6-ounce can tomato paste
1 teaspoon sugar
1 teaspoon vinegar
1 teaspoon chili powder
¾ teaspoon cumin
¾ teaspoon oregano
½ teaspoon salt
½ teaspoon basil
1 bay leaf
freshly ground pepper to taste
6 medium-size flour tortillas
6 eggs
1 to 1½ cups shredded jack cheese

Preheat oven to 350°.

EL PARADERO
220 West Manhattan
Santa Fe, New Mexico
87501
(505) 988-1177

MC/V
Moderate to expensive

A remodelled 1800 to 1850s adobe within walking distance of the plaza, this 12-room inn offers a hearty full-course breakfast, and wine and cheese in the afternoon.

In large skillet, sauté onion and garlic in oil until limp. Add chilies, stewed tomatoes, tomato sauce, tomato paste, sugar, vinegar, chili powder, cumin, oregano, salt, basil, bay leaf and pepper. Mix well and cover. Let simmer over low heat for at least 2 hours. If sauce gets too thick, add water. Refrigerate. At serving time, wrap tortillas in foil and warm while reheating sauce. Poach eggs. Place warm tortilla on oven-proof plate and place poached egg in center. Spoon sauce over egg to cover tortilla. Sprinkle cheese over all and place in oven until cheese is melted. Serves 6.

THE HANFORD HOUSE

Jimmy's Favorite Nut Bread

2 large eggs
2 cups brown sugar
3½ cups all-purpose flour
1 teaspoon baking soda

1 teaspoon baking powder
¼ teaspoon salt
1 cup chopped walnuts
1¼ cups buttermilk

Preheat oven to 350°. Butter two loaf pans.

Beat eggs, add sugar and mix well. In a separate bowl, sift together flour, baking soda, baking powder and salt. Stir walnuts into dry ingredients. Add dry ingredients alternately with the buttermilk to egg-sugar mixture. Batter will be stiff. Pour into pans, and level the tops. Bake approximately 50 minutes. Test for doneness. (A cake tester or toothpick should come out dry.) Cool 10 minutes in pans, then turn out onto racks. This heavy nutbread freezes well and is best sliced thin. Also delicious toasted and spread with butter or whipped cream cheese. Each loaf serves 8 to 10.

THE HANFORD HOUSE
Highway 49
3 Hanford Street
P.O. Box 847
Sutter Creek, California 95685
(209) 267-0747

MC/V
Moderate to expensive

This newly-built, 9-room inn is set in an historic California gold rush town.

THE TURNING POINT

Turning Point Breakfast Muffins

1 cup whole wheat flour
1½ cups raw bran
1 teaspoon baking powder
1 teaspoon baking soda
¾ cup raisins
1 egg, lightly beaten
1 tablespoon oil or melted butter

¾ cup milk
¾ cup apple juice
2 tablespoons maple syrup or honey
cinnamon to taste
12 walnut halves

Preheat oven to 375°. Butter 12 muffin tins.

Mix together whole wheat flour, bran, baking powder, baking soda and raisins. Add the remaining ingredients, stirring well to incorporate them evenly. Divide dough into the 12 muffin tins. Top with walnut halves. Bake for about 15 minutes or until muffins test done. Serve hot. Yields 12 muffins.

THE TURNING POINT
Route 23 & Lake Buel Road
R.D. 2, Box 140
Great Barrington, Massachusetts
01230
(413) 528-4777

No credit cards
Moderate

Located not far from Tanglewood and ski slopes, The Turning Point has a no-smoking policy and serves vegetarian wholegrain breakfasts.

North Carolina Applesauce Muffins

½ cup softened butter
1 cup sugar
1 egg
1 cup unsweetened
   applesauce
1½ teaspoons ground
   cinnamon

1 teaspoon ground allspice
½ teaspoon ground cloves
½ teaspoon salt
1 teaspoon baking soda
2 cups all-purpose flour
½ cup chopped nuts

Preheat oven to 350°. Butter 24 small muffin tins.

Cream butter and sugar. Add eggs one at a time. Stir in applesauce and spices. Sift together salt, soda and flour. Add to applesauce mixture and beat well. Stir in nuts. Fill muffin tins ⅔ full and bake for 8 to 10 minutes. Batter keeps well in refrigerator, and baked muffins freeze well (reheat before serving). Yields 24 small muffins.

HAVENSHIRE INN
Route 4, Box 455,
Cummings Road
Hendersonville,
North Carolina
28739
(704) 692-4097

MC/V
Moderate to expensive

A 6-room rural retreat on 40 acres overlooking the French Broad River, Havenshire Inn offers hiking, canoeing, fishing and swimming.

The Barnard Good House
Cape May, New Jersey

Two Meeting Street Inn
Charleston, South Carolina

THE GRAY WHALE INN

Vanilla Streusel Coffee Cake

3 cups all-purpose flour
1½ teaspoons baking
   powder
1½ teaspoons baking soda
¼ teaspoon salt
1½ cups softened butter
1½ cups sugar
3 eggs
1½ cups sour cream

1½ teaspoons vanilla
¾ cup firmly packed
   brown sugar
¾ cup chopped nuts
1½ teaspoons cinnamon
2 tablespoons vanilla
   mixed with 2 table-
   spoons water

Preheat oven to 325°. Butter 10″ tube pan.

Sift together flour, baking powder, baking soda and salt, and set aside. Combine butter and sugar in large bowl and beat until fluffy. Add eggs one at a time, beating well after each addition. Blend in sour cream and vanilla. Gradually add sifted dry ingredients and beat well. Combine brown sugar, nuts and cinnamon in a separate bowl. Turn ⅓ of the batter into the tube pan and sprinkle with ½ of the nut mixture. Repeat. Add remaining batter and spoon diluted vanilla over top. Bake 60 to 70 minutes. Cool completely before removing from pan. (Texture will be moist.) Makes one cake, which serves 10 to 12.

THE GREY WHALE INN

Apricot-Prune Coffee Cake

This recipe was a blue-ribbon winner at the 1983 Mendocino County (California) Apple Show and Fair.

BATTER:
¾ cup dried apricots
¾ cup pitted dried prunes
3 cups unsifted all-purpose
  flour
½ tablespoon baking
  powder
¾ teaspoon baking soda
¼ teaspoon salt
¾ cup softened butter
1½ cups sugar
4 eggs
½ tablespoon vanilla
1 cup sour cream

STREUSEL:
½ cup firmly packed light
  brown sugar
2 tablespoons softened
  butter
2 tablespoons al!-purpose
  flour
1 teaspoon cinnamon
2 tablespoons powdered
  sugar (optional)

Preheat oven to 350°. Butter a 10" tube pan and dust with flour.

Coarsely chop apricots and prunes. Toss to combine. Sift together flour, baking powder, baking soda and salt. Set aside. Beat butter until fluffy (about 3 minutes). Gradually beat in sugar, then eggs, one at a time. Add vanilla. Blend in flour mixture alternately with sour cream, beginning and ending with flour mixture. Blend just until batter is smooth. Gently fold in the prunes and apricots.

Mix together first four streusel ingredients with a fork until crumbly. (Will make approximately one cup of streusel.)

Turn ⅓ of the batter into the prepared tube pan, spreading evenly. Sprinkle with ⅓ of the streusel mixture. Repeat, layering the remaining batter and streusel twice. Bake 55 to 60 minutes, or until cake tester comes out clean. Let cool in pan about 20 minutes. Remove from pan to platter. Sift powdered sugar over top if desired. This cake can be served warm. Yields one cake, which serves 10 to 12.

GREY WHALE INN
615 North Main Street
Fort Bragg, California
95437
(707) 964-0640

MC/V/AE
Moderate to expensive

This historic north coast Californian landmark features ocean-view suites, antiques and an extensive art collection.

A N C H U C A

Overnight Coffee Cake

¾ cup softened butter
1 cup sugar
2 eggs
1 cup sour cream
2 cups all-purpose flour
1 teaspoon baking powder
1 teaspoon baking soda
½ teaspoon salt

1 teaspoon ground nutmeg
¾ cup firmly packed
  brown sugar
½ cup chopped walnuts
  or pecans
1 teaspoon ground
  cinnamon

Butter a 3″ by 9″ by 2″ baking pan and lightly dust with flour.

Cream butter and sugar until light and fluffy. Add eggs and sour cream, mixing well. Combine flour, baking powder, baking soda, salt and nutmeg. Add to batter and mix well. Pour into baking pan. In a separate bowl, combine brown sugar, nuts and cinnamon. Mix well and sprinkle evenly over batter. Cover and chill overnight.

In the morning, uncover and bake at 350° for 35 to 40 minutes, or until cake tests done. Serves 15.

ANCHUCA
1010 First East Street
Vicksburg, Mississippi
39180
(601) 636-4931

MC/V/AE
Very expensive

Guests at Anchuca can immerse themselves in Southern splendor, sipping mint juleps by the swimming pool, relaxing in antique-furnished bedrooms and enjoying breakfast in the inn's magnificent dining room.

S C H W E G M A N N   H O U S E

Coconut Breakfast Bread

2¾ cups all-purpose flour
1¼ cups toasted flaked
  coconut
¾ cup sugar
1 tablespoon baking
  powder

1 teaspoon salt
1½ cups milk
3 tablespoons melted butter
1 teaspoon coconut extract

Preheat oven to 350°. Butter and flour a 9″ by 5″ by 3″ pan.

Combine flour, coconut, sugar, baking powder and salt in a large bowl and make a well in the center of the mixture. Combine the remaining ingredients. Add the liquids to the dry mixture and stir until well moistened. Spoon into loaf pan. Bake for one hour or until tests done. Cool for 10 minutes in pan, then remove and cool completely on wire rack. Yields one loaf, which serves 8 to 10.

THE SCHWEGMANN
HOUSE
438 West Front Street
Washington, Missouri
63090
(314) 239-5025

MC/V
Moderate

This pre-Civil War building, with its 9 gracious antique-appointed rooms, sits on the banks of the Missouri River, just an hour's drive west of St. Louis.

Sutter Creek Inn,
Sutter Creek, California

T H E   A B B E Y

Sly Devil Eggs

6 hard-boiled eggs	¼ teaspoon dry mustard
¼ cup melted butter	1 (2½ ounce) can
½ teaspoon	deviled ham
Worcestershire sauce	3 scallions, minced

Preheat oven to 350°. Butter a 9″ casserole dish.

Cut eggs in half and remove yolks. Mix yolks with butter, Worcestershire sauce, mustard, ham and scallions, blending until smooth. Stuff mixture into egg-white halves. Arrange eggs in the casserole.

SAUCE:

¼ cup (½ stick) butter	salt and pepper to taste
¼ cup flour	English muffins
2 cups milk	

Melt the butter in a saucepan. Stir in the flour to form a paste and cook for a minute or two. Whisk in the milk and season with salt and pepper. Heat until thickened. Pour the sauce over the eggs and sprinkle with grated cheese. (This can be assembled ahead of time, refrigerated overnight, and heated before serving.)

Bake for 20 to 25 minutes. Serve over toasted English muffins. Serves 6.

THE ABBEY
Columbia Avenue and
Gurney Street
Cape May, New Jersey
08204
(609) 884-4506

MC/V
Expensive

The Abbey, in the historic resort community of Cape May, is located just one block from the Atlantic Ocean.

S E A F A I R   I N N

Gingerbread Muffins

½ cup sugar
2½ cups all-purpose flour
1½ teaspoons baking soda
1 teaspoon cinnamon
1 teaspoon ginger
½ teaspoon salt

¼ teaspoon nutmeg
1 cup chopped nuts
1 egg
1 cup molasses
1 cup buttermilk
½ cup melted butter

Preheat oven to 350°. Butter muffin tins.

Combine sugar, flour, baking soda, cinnamon, ginger, salt, nutmeg and nuts in a bowl. In a separate bowl, mix egg, molasses, buttermilk and melted butter, and add to the dry ingredients. Stir until just blended. Spoon into muffin tins and bake for 20 to 25 minutes. Test with a toothpick: muffins are done when it comes out clean. Can also be served warmed with whipped cream or ice cream as a dessert. Serves 12.

SEAFAIR INN
24 Shore Road
Ogunquit, Maine
03907
(207) 646-2181

MC/V
Moderate

Nestled in the tiny town of Ogunquit along Maine's rocky southern coast, the classic Seafair Inn has 20 antique-appointed rooms.

Part 2

BRUNCH

The Inn at Weston
Weston, Vermont

Brunch

This felicitous combination of breakfast and lunch should be slowly savored on a lazy morning. Whether enjoyed in an inn or your own home, the ingredients are the same: good food, pleasant surroundings and good conversation.

The Union Hotel in Benicia (an artist's colony not far from San Francisco) is a mecca for lovers of American cuisine. Brunch guests delight in scrapple, homemade sausage, grits, red plaid hash and scrumptious cream biscuits.

Brunch can be served as individually ordered entrées or as a buffet—a splendid idea for entertaining at home. Gramma's B & B Inn in Berkeley, California, presents so many buffet dishes that it's difficult to decide where to begin. Will it be green salad, crudités, paté, pasta salad, shirred eggs, sausage, home-fried potatoes, or a bit of each? You can greet your guests with a big pitcher of Bloody Marys and then slowly unveil the morning's delights. Whether you serve Shrimp Scampi Bicard, Crustless Quiche, Dill Bread or Buttermilk Pie, it's sure to be a meal to be remembered.

JULIAN'S AT THE NEW SHERIDAN

Spinach Frittata

2 eggs
½ cup cooked, drained
   and chopped spinach
2 tablespoons water

¼ cup warm tomato
   sauce
3 strips Mozzarella cheese

Combine eggs, spinach and water. Pour into hot, greased omelette pan and cook over medium heat until egg mixture sets. Remove from heat. Ladle sauce over cooked eggs. Place strips of cheese over top and place under broiler until Mozzarella melts. Serves 2.

NEW SHERIDAN HOTEL
231 Colorado Avenue
Telluride, Colorado
81435
(303) 728-4351

MC/V/AE
Moderate

The New Sheridan Hotel of Telluride, a National Historic Landmark, is situated in one of Colorado's most beautiful towns.

CITY HOTEL

Shrimp-Shirred Eggs

3 tablespoons clarified
   butter
8 eggs
1 large shallot, chopped
1 cup brut champagne
1½ pounds frozen or fresh
   shrimp, peeled and
   deveined

3 cups heavy cream
¼ pound (1 stick)
   unsalted butter
8 olive rounds
salt and pepper to taste

Preheat oven to 350°. Butter a shallow, oven-proof casserole dish large enough to hold 8 eggs in a single layer.

Crack eggs in the casserole, being careful not to break the yolks. Dot yolks with 1 tablespoon clarified butter and bake uncovered in oven until the yolks are set.

Heat remaining 2 tablespoons clarified butter in a large skillet. Sauté the chopped shallots lightly in the butter. Add champagne and reduce by half. Add the shrimp and cook gently for 2 to 3 minutes. Remove shrimp with a slotted spoon and keep warm. Increase heat under skillet and reduce juices to a thin glaze. Blend in cream and simmer until mixture thickens, about 20 to 30 minutes. Remove from heat and whisk in ¼ pound (1 stick) butter, a tablespoon at a time. Stir in the reserved shrimp, season to taste and pour over the shirred eggs. Garnish with olive slices. Serves 4.

CITY HOTEL
P.O. Box 1870
Columbia, California
95310
(209) 532-1479

MC/V
Expensive

Located in an historic gold rush town which is now a state park, the City Hotel's dining room and saloon serve as a training ground for students enrolled in the hotel management and culinary program of a nearby college.

CAPTAIN MEY'S INN

Quiche Mey

6 eggs
2 cups heavy cream
½ cup fresh bread crumbs
½ teaspoon salt

¼ teaspoon nutmeg
2 tablespoons frozen
orange juice concentrate
1 cup chopped spinach

Preheat oven to 350°. Butter a quiche dish.

Beat eggs and cream together. Stir in bread crumbs, salt, nutmeg, orange juice and spinach. Pour into quiche dish. Bake 40 minutes in oven or 20 minutes in microwave. Makes one quiche, which serves 8.

CAPTAIN MEY'S INN
202 Ocean Street
Cape May, New Jersey
08204
(609) 884-7793 and
(609) 884-9637

MC/V
Expensive

Named after this resort town's Dutch explorer-founder, the inn keeps the heritage of Holland alive, with a Delft Blue collection, Dutch artifacts and imported cheeses.

WHITE CLOUD SYLVAN RETREAT

White Cloud Cashew Soup

3 cups water or soup stock
1 cup cashew pieces
1 scant teaspoon curry
powder
1 teaspoon salt

1 heaping teaspoon
poultry seasoning
4 teaspoons chives for
garnish
paprika to taste for garnish

Heat first five ingredients to boiling. Put in blender and blend until smooth. Reheat briefly and serve sprinkled with chopped chives and paprika. Yields 4 cups or 4 servings.

WHITE CLOUD SYLVAN RETREAT
Route 447
Newfoundland, Pennsylvania
18445
(717) 676-3162

MC/V/AE/DC
Inexpensive

This retreat of 50 wooded acres offers a swimming pool, tennis court, peace of mind and meatless natural-foods cooking.

Cleftstone Manor
Bar Harbor, Maine

THE GLENBOROUGH INN

Momma's Egg Casserole

little soggy

8 slices bread	4 ounces chopped chilies
7 eggs	3 cups grated sharp cheddar
2½ cups milk	
1 teaspoon oregano	3 cups grated jack cheese
½ teaspoon minced garlic	1 avocado, sliced
1½ teaspoons salt	½ cup sour cream

essential

The night before, place slices of bread in a 9″ by 12″ buttered casserole dish. (Can also be placed in individual casseroles.) Spread the chilies over the bread. Mix together the eggs, milk, oregano, garlic and salt. Pour the egg mixture over the chilies. Sprinkle the cheeses over the entire dish. Cover and refrigerate overnight.

The next morning, preheat oven to 325°. Bake for 50 minutes or until puffy and barely set. (Bake individual casseroles for 15 minutes.) Serve immediately with avocado slices and sour cream garnish. Serves 8 to 12.

GLENBOROUGH INN AND COTTAGE
1327 Bath Street
Santa Barbara, California 93101
(805) 966-0589

MC/V
Moderate to very expensive

In the seaside resort community of Santa Barbara, the Glenborough Inn and Cottage has 8 antique-appointed rooms and suites and serves a full breakfast in bed.

DANA'S AT PISTACHIO COVE

Pistachio Cove's Puffy Cloud Brunchwiches

8 slices firm bread	½ cup ricotta cheese
butter to cover the 8 slices bread	1 teaspoon each minced onion and parsley
4 slices Swiss cheese	½ cup orange marmalade
4 slices ham	¼ cup pineapple preserves
4 eggs	2 tablespoons Galliano liqueur
1 cup milk	

Preheat oven to 375°. Butter an 8″ by 8″ by 2″ baking dish.

Butter bread. Place 4 slices, buttered-side down, in baking dish. Top with cheese slices and ham. Cover with remaining bread slices, buttered-side up. Beat together eggs, milk, ricotta cheese, onion and parsley. Pour over sandwiches. Bake for 30 minutes, or until puffy and golden. Stir together marmalade, preserves and liqueur to make a topping. Pass topping around table and allow guests to help themselves. This recipe goes well with a fresh fruit compote and granola-topped coffee cake. Serves 4.

DANA'S AT PISTACHIO COVE
R.F.D. 5
Lakeville, Massachusetts 02346
(617) 763-2383

No credit cards
Inexpensive

The elegant but inexpensive Dana's at Pistachio Cove on Massachusetts' Lake Apponequet is a venue for boating, fishing, swimming and total relaxation.

HOLIDAY INN

Sherried Crab Quiche

9" pie crust (see
  following recipe
4 tablespoons softened
  butter
2 cups heavy cream
4 eggs
1 teaspoon salt
¼ pound shredded Swiss
  cheese

2 tablespoons minced
  onion
two 6-ounce packages
  frozen snow crab,
  thawed and drained
2 tablespoons dry sherry
⅛ teaspoon Cayenne
  pepper

Preheat oven to 425°. Prepare pie crust and line a 9" pie plate with the crust. Spread crust with one tablespoon softened butter and set aside.

In a medium bowl, whisk together cream, eggs and salt until well blended. Stir in cheese. Over medium heat, melt remaining three tablespoons butter, add the onions and cook until softened (about 5 minutes). Stir onions, crab, sherry and Cayenne pepper into the egg-cream mixture. Pour into buttered pie crust (see following recipe). Bake for 15 minutes. Lower oven to 325° and bake 35 minutes longer, or until knife inserted in center comes out clean. Serves 8.

BUTTER PIE CRUST:
4 tablespoons butter
1 cup unsifted flour

1 egg yolk
5 teaspoons ice water

Cut butter into flour until mixture forms coarse crumbs. Lightly stir in egg yolk with a fork. Add water, a little at a time, and stir until pastry clings together. Form it into a ball and refrigerate for at least one hour before rolling it out.

HOLIDAY INN
Route 16A
Intervale, New Hampshire
03845
(603) 356-9772

MC/V/AE
Expensive

In the heart of New Hampshire's White Mountains is the Holiday Inn, the place for traditional hospitality and old-fashioned relaxation.

The National House Inn
Marshall, Michigan

Galer Place
Seattle, Washington

F O X   S T A N D   I N N

Eggs à la Jean

This recipe is great for using up leftovers.

2 tablespoons butter	*1 tablespoon sherry*
¼ cup chopped onion	*¼ teaspoon tarragon*
¼ cup cubed baked	*¼ teaspoon basil*
* potatoes*	*salt and pepper to taste*
¼ cup broccoli pieces	*¼ cup cream*
¼ cup diced green pepper	*¼ cup shredded cheddar*
¼ cup ham chunks	* cheese*
1 clove garlic, minced	*8 eggs*

Preheat oven to 350°. Butter a small casserole or 4 boat dishes.

Melt butter in a sauté pan. Sauté onion, potatoes, broccoli, peppers, ham and garlic until heated through. Add sherry and seasonings to taste, then mix in cream and cheese. Stir until cheese melts. Line a casserole or 4 dishes with this mixture, and top with eggs (2 per individual boat dish). Bake until egg whites are firm. Serve this dish with fresh fruit. Serves 4.

FOX STAND INN
Route 14
Royalton, Vermont
05068

No credit cards
Inexpensive

The Fox Stand Inn and restaurant is an historic stagecoach stop built in 1818 on the banks of the White River.

Cauliflower Custard
in Swiss Chard Leaves

1 bunch Swiss chard
1 head cauliflower
1 onion, chopped
1 clove garlic, chopped
1½ cups cream or half-
    and-half
7 eggs

½ cup grated Parmesan
    cheese
½ cup grated mozzarella
    cheese
salt, pepper and nutmeg
    to taste

Preheat oven to 350°. Butter a ring mold.

Blanch the chard by placing leaves in a large pot of boiling water for a minute or so. Run under cold water, then drain on paper towels. Line ring mold with the leaves of chard, flopping the extra over the outside (you will fold them in later). Chop and cook the cauliflower. While cauliflower is cooking, sauté the onion and garlic. Set aside. Purée cauliflower in a blender or food processor with some of the cream. Add eggs and blend well. Add onion and garlic. Add cheeses, the remaining cream, and seasonings. Mix well. Pour custard into the lined mold, lapping the leaves over the top and set pan in a *bain marie* filled with ½" of water. Cover the top of the mold with buttered wax paper. Bake for 25 to 30 minutes or until custard tests done. Loosen edges right away, but allow dish to stand for at least 5 minutes before turning mold out. Can be served hot or cold. Serves 6 to 8.

GRAMMA'S BED &
BREAKFAST INN
2740 Telegraph Avenue
Berkeley, California
94705
(415) 549-2145

MC/V
Expensive

Just a short walk from the University of California campus, Gramma's offers a Sunday champagne brunch.

Sunflower Special

5 eggs
¼ cup all-purpose flour
½ teaspoon baking
    powder
¼ teaspoon salt
½ teaspoon chili powder
1 cup cottage cheese

½ pound jack cheese,
    grated
¼ cup butter, melted
½ cup sour cream
one 4-ounce can diced
    green chilies, drained
sour cream for garnish

Preheat oven to 350°.

Beat eggs. Add remaining ingredients, beating after each addition. Pour into 6 buttered ramekins. Bake 30 minutes. Serve immediately with a dollop of sour cream. Serves 6.

BIG YELLOW
SUNFLOWER
235 Sky Oaks
Angwin, California
94508
(707) 965-3885

No credit cards
Expensive to very
expensive

This small one-suite bed and breakfast located just above northern California's Napa Valley offers a private retreat with very bountiful breakfasts.

ROSE   VICTORIAN   INN

Cheese Strata

12 slices bread, cubed
2¼ cups grated cheese
3 cups milk
12 eggs
6 tablespoons melted
   butter

¾ teaspoon dry mustard
chopped ham (optional)
chopped green chilies
   (optional)

Preheat oven to 350°. Butter a baking dish.

Layer dish with bread and cheese, ending with cheese. (Chopped ham or green chilies may be layered into the bread and cheese for variety.) Combine milk, eggs, melted butter and mustard in blender for about 10 seconds. Pour over bread/cheese mixture and refrigerate overnight. Bake until firm in the center, about 45 to 60 minutes.

ROSE VICTORIAN INN
789 Valley Road
Arroyo Grande, California
93420
(805) 481-5566

MC/V/AE
Expensive

A majestic 98-year-old mansion on the edge of the Pacific, the Rose Victorian Inn is noted for beautiful gardens and gourmet meals served in the dining room under its crystal chandelier.

THE   BRIGGS   HOUSE

Briggs House Frittata

4 tablespoons butter
1½ cups chopped green
   onions
2 cloves garlic, minced
2 cups finely chopped
   Swiss chard, spinach,
   broccoli or mushrooms
½ teaspoon basil
½ teaspoon oregano

½ teaspoon thyme
12 eggs
1 teaspoon salt
¼ teaspoon pepper
½ cup heavy or sour
   cream
2 cups shredded Swiss
   cheese
1 cup Parmesan cheese

Preheat oven to 350°.

Melt butter in a skillet. Sauté green onions and garlic until onion is limp. Add the vegetables and cook until they are just heated through (about 3 minutes). Remove from heat and stir in herbs. Lightly beat the eggs with salt, pepper and cream. Stir in 1½ cups of Swiss cheese and ½ cup Parmesan cheese along with the vegetables. Bake for 30 to 40 minutes. Remove from oven and sprinkle remaining Swiss and Parmesan cheeses over the top. Cook for 5 more minutes to melt the cheese and lightly brown the top. Cool slightly and cut. Serves 8 to 10.

THE BRIGGS HOUSE
2209 Capitol Avenue
Sacramento, California
95816
(916) 441-3214

MC/V/AE
Expensive

Located just a short walk from California's State Capitol building, the elegant Briggs House offers its guests a hot tub, bicycles, complimentary wine and occasional entertainment.

SNOWVILLAGE INN

Tomato Soup with Cognac

3 pounds ripe tomatoes
    (canned tomatoes may
    be substituted if
    necessary)
1 large onion
3 ounces butter
1 teaspoon fresh basil or
    ¼ teaspoon dried basil

1 pint heavy or whipping
    cream
1 teaspoon brown sugar
4 to 5 tablespoons cognac
salt and pepper to taste

Scald tomatoes and slip off their skins. Chop them coarsely. Chop onion. Melt butter in a large soup pot. Sauté onion till brown and add tomatoes and basil. Let simmer over low heat for one hour. Heat cream and sugar in another pot just until ready to boil. Stirring quickly, pour the cream into the tomatoes. Add cognac, season well with salt and pepper and serve. Serves 6.

SNOWVILLAGE INN
Foss Mountain Road
Snowville, New Hampshire
03849
(603) 447-2818

All major credit cards
Expensive

This secluded inn offers its guests spectacular views, delicious meals, a friendly atmosphere, tennis, and cross-country ski trails right outside the door.

SAGEBRUSH INN

Chili Rellenos

Rellenos may be served as an entrée or as an accompaniment to other Mexican foods.

enough cooking oil to fill
    deep fryer
12 to 16 chilies (fresh or
    canned)
½ to ¾ pound mellow
    cheese, such as Colby,
    Monterrey jack, or
    other mild cheese
4 cups flour

2 eggs
1½ cups beer
2 cups lukewarm water
½ teaspoon ground cumin
½ teaspoon salt
½ teaspoon Maggi liquid
    seasoning
1½ cups flour

Preheat 5 to 6 inches of oil in deep fryer to 350° to 375°.

Split the chilies lengthwise down the top and clean and remove seeds. Cut cheese into strips 4" long by 1" wide. Stuff chilies with cheese strips. With an electric mixer, blend flour, eggs, beer, water, cumin, salt, and Maggi.

Dip the stuffed rellenos in additional flour, then in the batter. Fry until golden brown. Makes 12 to 16.

SAGEBRUSH INN
P.O. Box 1566
Taos, New Mexico 87571
(505) 758-2254

MC/V/AE/DC
Moderate

This 16-room adobe inn is furnished with hand-carved Southwest furniture and little kiva fireplaces.

THE INN AT WESTON

Salmon Roulade with Dijon Cream
or Lemon Curry Sauce

Preheat oven to 400°. Grease a 12″ by 18″ baking pan with 3 tablespoons cooking oil.

ROULADE:

7 eggs	2 tablespoons sour cream
4 tablespoons dried dill weed	1 extra egg white dash of cream of tartar
¼ cup all-purpose flour	

Separate eggs. Mix yolks with dill, flour and sour cream. Set aside. Beat 8 egg whites until fluffy. Add cream of tartar and beat until stiff. Stir some whites into yolk mixture to lighten, then fold in remaining whites. Put baking pan in oven for 5 minutes. Remove pan and spread evenly with egg mixture. Bake for 10 minutes or until it is golden and sides begin to pull away from pan. Cover pan with a clean towel and a baking sheet. Flip pan over so that cake inverts onto towel.

FILLING:

1 pound fresh salmon, cooked and flaked	1 cup grated Gruyère cheese
½ cup sour cream	⅓ cup mayonnaise
	½ teaspoon salt

Mix salmon, sour cream, grated Gruyère, mayonnaise and salt to make the filling. Spread on cake. Roll cake jelly-roll fashion, using the towel to help. Refrigerate, wrapped tightly in plastic wrap, until ready to use.

SAUCE:

4 tablespoons butter	curry sauce, substitute 3
4 tablespoons all-purpose flour	to 4 tablespoons lemon juice and 1½ teaspoons
½ cup dry white wine	curry powder)
1 cup fish stock	2 tablespoons fresh chives
1 tablespoon Dijon mustard (for lemon	½ cup whipping cream

Prepare sauce by melting butter and stirring in flour to make a golden-colored roux. Add wine, fish stock, and sauce flavorings (mustard or lemon juice and curry). Cook for 10 to 15 minutes over low heat. Whisk in cream and cook until slightly thickened. Stir in chives and season with salt and pepper.

Before serving, preheat oven to 325°. Remove plastic wrap from roulade and place on buttered baking sheet. Top with some sauce or grated Gruyère cheese. Heat in oven for about 25 minutes or until heated through. Serves 8.

THE INN AT WESTON
Route 100, Box 56
Weston, Vermont
05161
(802) 824-5804

No credit cards
Moderate

The innkeepers at this 13-room inn foster friendships among their guests and prepare creative country cuisine that has been featured in *Gourmet* Magazine.

A S A   R A N S O M   H O U S E

Caraway and Sour Cream Soup

4 cups chicken stock
¼ cup chicken fat or ⅛
    cup butter and ⅛ cup
    cooking oil
2 cups medium-dice
    onions
1 cup medium-dice celery

1 cup medium-dice carrots
salt and pepper
1 tablespoon caraway
    seeds
½ cup all-purpose flour
1 cup sour cream
½ cup milk

Heat the chicken stock. In a separate 3-quart saucepan, melt chicken fat or heat butter and oil mixture. Sauté onions, celery and carrots. Season lightly with salt and pepper. Add caraway seeds. Sauté until the onion is transparent. Reduce heat and add flour, stirring constantly so as not to scorch. Cook for 5 to 8 minutes to bind the flour and fat. Gradually add hot chicken stock, stirring to dissolve the roux (mixture of flour and fat). Bring the soup to a boil, then reduce heat and let simmer.

In a separate bowl, mix sour cream with one cup of hot soup and stir vigorously to prevent curdling. Pour this mixture back into the soup and heat, taking care not to allow soup to boil. Finally, add milk and season with salt and pepper to taste. Serve hot. Yields 2 quarts or servings for 8.

ASA RANSOM HOUSE
10529 Main Street
Clarence, New York
14031
(716) 759-2315

No credit cards
Moderate

This 4-room village inn includes a library, gift shop, taproom and herb garden.

P E T I T E   A U B E R G E

Crustless Quiche

3 tablespoons butter
2 cups chopped vegetables
    (onions, green pepper,
    broccoli, cauliflower,
    asparagus or other as
    desired)
1 cup grated Swiss cheese

6 eggs
1½ cups heavy cream
½ teaspoon salt
¼ teaspoon pepper
pinch each of nutmeg and
    garlic powder
Parmesan cheese to taste

Preheat oven to 350°. Liberally butter a quiche dish.

Layer vegetables and Swiss cheese in dish halfway to the top. Lightly beat together eggs, cream, salt, pepper and spices. Pour over vegetables and cheese. Bake for 30 minutes. Remove from oven, sprinkle Parmesan cheese on top and return to oven for 15 minutes more.

PETITE AUBERGE
863 Bush Street
San Francisco, California
94108
(415) 928-6000

MC/V/AE
Very expensive

The ambience of the French countryside has found its way to downtown San Francisco. Petite Auberge, with its 26 rooms, is filled with antiques, flowers and friendliness.

DUNBAR HOUSE, 1880

Chili, Cheese, Sausage Trio

two 4-ounce cans whole
  chilies
1 pound link sausages
½ pound Monterrey jack
  cheese
1 pound cheddar cheese
one 13-ounce can
  evaporated milk

2 to 3 tablespoons
  all-purpose flour
1 teaspoon baking powder
8 eggs, beaten lightly
one 8-ounce can tomato
  sauce

Preheat oven to 350°. Butter a 3-quart casserole dish.

Cut chilies into strips. Cook and quarter sausages. Layer chilies, sausages and cheese in the casserole dish. Mix milk, flour, baking powder and beaten eggs and pour over layers. Bake 30 to 40 minutes. Drizzle tomato sauce over and bake 10 minutes more. Let set 10 minutes before cutting and serving. Serves 8 to 10.

DUNBAR HOUSE
P.O. Box 1375
Murphys, California
95247
(209) 728-2897

No credit cards
Moderate

The Italianate-Victorian historic Dunbar House is located in a gold rush town in the foothills of the Sierras.

Snowvillage Inn
Snowville, New Hampshire

The Kenwood Inn
St. Augustine, Florida

BED & BREAKFAST, INC.

Red Beans and Rice

In New Orleans, this dish is traditionally served on Monday (washday), because it is slow cooking and takes little attention on a busy day. It is traditionally served with salad and garlic bread.

1 pound dry kidney beans
   or other red beans
a splash of oil
1 large onion, chopped
¼ cup celery, minced
¼ cup chopped bell
   pepper
3 cloves garlic, minced

½ pound salt pork, sliced
   (or seasoning ham or
   ham hock)
8 to 10 cups water
1 bay leaf
salt, pepper and Tabasco
   to taste
4 cups hot cooked rice

Cover beans in water and soak overnight, or boil 2 minutes and allow to stand for 1 hour. Drain. In a large cooking pot, sauté the vegetables in oil until soft. Add beans, salt pork or ham, water and bay leaf. Cook 1½ to 2 hours, stirring occasionally, crushing some beans to thicken the liquid. Spoon over rice. Serves 6 to 8.

BED & BREAKFAST, INC.
1236 Decatur Street
New Orleans, Louisiana
70116
(504) 525-4640

No credit cards
Inexpensive to expensive

This reservation service organization specializes in matching its guests with suitable rooms in private guest houses in the New Orleans vicinity. Accommodation possibilities include rooms in a French Quarter house beside a patio and swimming pool, in the home of a writer or artist, and in a residential neighborhood near Lake Pontchartrain.

OLDE TOWN FARM LODGE

Carrot Soup

3 tablespoons butter
6 large carrots, peeled and
    sliced
2 medium onions,
    chopped
1 large potato, peeled and
    diced

4 cups beef broth
½ teaspoon sugar
salt and pepper to taste
parsley or chervil (6 sprigs
    or 3 teaspoons chopped)

Melt butter in a heavy 3-quart saucepan and add carrots, onions and potatoes. Cook over medium heat till lightly browned (about 15 minutes), stirring occasionally. Add beef broth and sugar. Season with salt and pepper to taste. Heat just to boiling point, then reduce heat to low. Cover and cook 15 minutes or until vegetables are tender. Whisk in blender until smooth. Return to saucepan and reheat briefly. Garnish with parsley or chervil. Serves 6.

THE OLDE TOWN
FARM LODGE
Route 10
Gassetts, Vermont
05143
(802) 875-2346

MC/V/AE
Moderate

This classic Vermont country inn has a pond, a piano and a painstakingly restored spiral staircase.

LA BORDE HOUSE

Quinney's Bean Soup

1 pound pinto beans,
    soaked in advance
½ cup salt pork, diced
1 cup minced onion
½ cup minced bell
    peppers
1 large tomato, finely
    chopped
1 tablespoon minced
    cilantro (or coriander),
    chopped fine

1 Serrano pepper, minced
½ tablespoon freshly
    ground black pepper
½ tablespoon ground
    cumin
3 garlic cloves, minced
salt to taste

Using a 5-quart saucepan, bring beans and salt pork to a boil. Lower to moderate heat and continue cooking for 1½ hours. Stir in onions, bell peppers, tomatoes, cilantro and Serrano pepper. Mix garlic and seasonings together and add to soup. Cook for one more hour, stirring occasionally. Adjust seasonings to taste. Serves 6.

LA BORDE HOUSE
601 East Main Street
Rio Grande, Texas
78582
(512) 487-5101

MC/V/AE
Moderate

Located deep in south Texas, the La Borde House is a blend of old and new, with 8 antique-appointed rooms and 13 in modern style.

Eggplant St. Claire

cooking oil, enough for
   deep frying
1 cup all-purpose flour
egg wash (5 eggs beaten
   with small amount of
   water, a pinch of salt
   and pepper)
1 cup bread crumbs
4 eggplant halves, peeled
   and hollowed
2 ounces crabmeat,
   picked over
1 tablespoon heavy cream
pinch of seafood
   seasoning
minced garlic to taste
1 cup chopped parsley
1 pint heavy cream

1 pint oyster liquid
   (canned, if necessary)
chablis or other white
   wine, to taste
chicken base to taste
pinch of thyme
⅓ cup each of minced
   green onions, yellow
   onions, carrots, green
   bell peppers, celery and
   turnips
1 teaspoon Worcestershire
   Sauce
½ cup water
3 tablespoons cornstarch
8 oysters
4 peeled shrimp
chopped parsley for
   garnish

Fill deep fryer 5 to 6 inches deep with cooking oil. Preheat cooking oil to 320°.

Flour eggplant halves, dip in egg wash and roll in bread crumbs. Deep fry for 5 minutes, turning once. In a saucepan, mix together crabmeat, one tablespoon heavy cream, seafood seasoning (see following recipe), garlic and chopped parsley, and heat until hot. In another saucepan, bring 1 pint heavy cream and oyster liquid to a boil. Add white wine, chicken base, garlic, thyme, green onions, yellow onions, carrots, peppers, celery, turnips and Worcestershire Sauce and continue cooking over low heat. Add water to cornstarch to make a paste. Add cornstarch paste to oyster sauce, stirring over heat until sauce is thickened. Add oysters and shrimp to sauce. Remove from heat. Set deep-fried eggplant on individual plates. Fill each eggplant half with the hot crab filling and top with oyster sauce. Sprinkle with chopped parsley. Make sure each serving includes 2 oysters and 1 shrimp. Serves 4.

THE COLUMNS

Seafood Seasoning

2½ ounces salt
1 ounce thyme
1 ounce oregano
¾ ounce black pepper

2 ounces paprika
2 ounces granulated garlic
½ ounce Cayenne pepper

Combine all and store in a tightly covered container.

THE INN AT MANCHESTER

Fresh Crab Casserole

1 pound fresh crab meat
½ teaspoon salt
½ teaspoon pepper
1 tablespoon chopped
  parsley
1 teaspoon minced onion
1 cup heavy cream or
  half-and-half

1½ cups mayonnaise
4 hard-boiled eggs, cut in
  chunks
2 slices homemade or
  good quality white
  bread, cubed

Preheat oven to 350°. Butter a casserole dish.

Combine first 8 ingredients. Put in casserole. Sprinkle cubes of bread over the top. Bake for 40 to 45 minutes. Serves 4.

Herbed Cream Cheese

1 clove garlic, mashed
8 ounces cream cheese
4 ounces whipped
  sweet butter
⅛ teaspoon pepper

⅛ teaspoon thyme
⅛ teaspoon basil
⅛ teaspoon marjoram
⅛ teaspoon dill
¼ teaspoon oregano

Beat all ingredients together thoroughly. Chill 24 hours. Remove from refrigerator to soften for easy spreading. Serve with crackers or bagel chips. Serves 4.

THE COLUMNS
3811 Saint Charles Avenue
New Orleans, Louisiana
70115
(504) 899-9308

MC/V/AE
Expensive

Built in 1883 in the Garden District, The Columns has for years been one of New Orleans' finest small hotels and is listed in the National Register of Historic Places.

THE INN AT
MANCHESTER
Route 7
Manchester, Vermont
05254
(802) 362-1793

AE
Moderate

This 15-room inn is in the heart of a popular skiing area, and its swimming pool makes it a summer escape as well. The owner is also the chef.

Pudding Creek Inn
Fort Bragg, California

THE OLEMA INN

Smoked Trout and Celery Root Salad

2 cups grated celery root
    immersed in a lemon-
    water bath
one 6-ounce smoked
    trout*
⅓ cup homemade
    mayonnaise
1 tablespoon plus 1
    teaspoon grated
    horseradish
1 small Red Delicious
    apple, diced and
    immersed in a lemon-
    water bath

¼ teaspoon salt
4 butter lettuce leaves
fresh black pepper
½ small red onion, thinly
    sliced
⅓ cup coarsely-chopped
    toasted pecans

Blanch celery root in a large pot of rapidly-boiling salted water for 45 seconds, then plunge immediately into ice water to stop the cooking process. Drain and chill. Flake trout from the bone and refrigerate. Combine the mayonnaise and horseradish. Drain the diced apple. In a bowl, combine celery root, trout and drained apple. Add salt and toss well. Add mayonnaise. Toss again. Taste, and use more salt if needed (the saltiness of the trout will vary). Arrange on chilled plates lined with butter lettuce leaves. Grind fresh pepper on top of each salad. Garnish with onion slices and a sprinkling of toasted pecans. Serves 4.

*Olema Inn's Drew Spangler uses alderwood-smoked trout.

THE OLEMA INN

Dungeness Crab Lasagna

1 pound ricotta cheese
¼ cup sour cream
½ cup minced parsley
1 pound Dungeness crab
  meat, picked over
1 teaspoon salt
3 teaspoons minced garlic
freshly ground pepper

½ pound fresh spinach
  lasagna noodles
1½ cups béchamel sauce
1¼ pound grated
  Mozzarella cheese
1 cup grated Parmesan
  cheese

Preheat oven to 350°. Butter a 9″ by 13″ baking pan.

Combine ricotta, sour cream, parsley, crab meat, salt, one teaspoon minced garlic and a generous amount of pepper, and set aside. Cook pasta in rapidly-boiling salted water, until it is three-quarters cooked. Remove from water and place in cold water until ready to use. Add the remaining 2 teaspoons of garlic to the béchamel sauce.

In the baking pan, layer the lasagna as follows: sauce, pasta, sauce, half of the Mozzarella, pasta, sauce, ricotta, pasta, sauce, remaining Mozzarella and the Parmesan cheese. Cover with foil and bake for 30 minutes. Uncover during the final 10 minutes to brown the top. This may be made ahead and reheated before serving. Serves 12.

THE OLEMA INN
10000 Sir Francis Drake
  Boulevard
Olema, California
94950
(415) 663-8441

MC/V
Expensive

At the entrance to Point Reyes National Seashore just north of San Francisco, the century-old 3-room Olema is noted for its seafood.

CHALET SUZANNE

Shrimp Suzanne with Dill

½ cup sour cream
½ cup mayonnaise
½ cup chopped fresh
  cucumber, peeled and
  seeded
⅓ cup minced onion
1½ tablespoons fresh
  chopped dill
1½ teaspoons lemon juice

garlic to taste
salt and pepper
8 drops Tabasco
¼ teaspoon caraway
  seeds
1 pound shrimp (25 to 30
  count), cooked, peeled
  and cleaned
bibb lettuce

Mix first 10 ingredients together to make a sauce. Stir in shrimp. Mix well and chill. Serve on a bed of bibb lettuce, either as individual servings or in a lettuce-lined bowl. Serves 4 to 6.

CHALET SUZANNE
P.O. Drawer AC
Lake Wales, Florida
33859-9003
(813) 676-6011

All major credit cards
Expensive

With 30 rooms nestled on a private estate in central Florida, the Chalet Suzanne boasts its own lake, a swimming pool, private airstrip and multi-award-winning restaurant.

THE CROWN HOTEL

Shrimp Scampi Caribbean

2 cups sliced peeled
  tomatoes
1 cup tomato purée
2 teaspoons Italian
  seasoning
salt and pepper to taste
16 to 20 jumbo shrimp
  scampi, peeled and
  cleaned
1 cup seasoned flour
2 tablespoons butter

2 tablespoons chopped
  bell peppers
2 tablespoons chopped
  onion
1 peach, peeled, pitted and
  roughly chopped
2 pineapple rings, roughly
  chopped
2 jiggers dark rum
12 ounces heavy cream
2 teaspoons Worcester-
  shire Sauce

Combine first 4 ingredients in a saucepan and cook over high heat for 10 minutes, or until liquid is cooked off, to make tomatoes concassées. Leftover tomatoes concassées will keep, covered, in the refrigerator for several days and freeze well.

Dredge scampi in seasoned flour. Melt butter in shallow pan. Cook scampi in butter for one minute. Remove scampi from pan and keep warm. Add peppers, onions, peach and pineapple to pan. Sauté for one minute. Add rum, cream, 2 tablespoons tomatoes concassée and Worcestershire sauce. Simmer a minute longer. Return scampi to pan and bring to a boil. Serve with boiled rice. Serves 2.

Shrimp Scampi Bicard

16 to 20 jumbo shrimp
  scampi, peeled and
  cleaned
1 cup seasoned flour
2 tablespoons butter
2 tablespoons sliced
  mushrooms
2 tablespoons peeled,
  diced tomatoes

2 tablespoons finely diced
  onions
4 ounces dry white wine
4 ounces heavy cream
2 teaspoons curry powder
2 tablespoons peeled,
  chopped mango

Dredge scampi in seasoned flour. Sauté in butter for one minute. Remove from pan and keep warm. Add mushrooms, tomatoes and onions to pan. Sauté for one minute. Stir in remaining ingredients and simmer for another minute. Return scampi to pan. Bring to a boil. Spoon over boiled rice. Serves 2.

THE CROWN HOTEL
109 North Seminole
  Avenue
Inverness, Florida
32650
(904) 344-5555

V/AE/CB/DC
Expensive

The Crown Hotel began as a general store over a century ago and has evolved into a 34-room inn with swimming pool and award-winning restaurant.

Garratt Mansion
Alameda, California

PARADISE RANCH INN

Paradise Grilled Salmon
with Tarragon Mayonnaise

6 salmon steaks (about ½
   pound each, cut 1"
   thick)
2 cups mayonnaise
¼ cup chopped fresh
   tarragon (or ¼ cup
   chopped fresh parsley
   combined with 2
   teaspoons crumbled
   dried tarragon)
3 tablespoons finely
   minced green or red
   onion

2 tablespoons fresh
   lemon juice
2 tablespoons
   chopped capers
¼ teaspoon pepper
salt to taste
lemon or lime slices or
   fresh tarragon sprigs for
   garnish

Combine all ingredients (except salmon and garnishes) in large bowl and blend well. Cover and chill 2 to 24 hours.

Arrange rack over grill or broiler pan about 5 inches from heat source. Brush rack with oil. Preheat coals or broiler.

Place salmon steaks on rack and spread top of each with 2 to 2½ tablespoons tarragon mayonnaise. Broil 6 minutes. Turn fish over on grill, mayonnaise-side down, and spread with another 2 to 2½ tablespoons mayonnaise. Broil 4 to 6 more minutes, until tip of knife pierced into middle of steak near center meets little resistance. (Fish should be barely opaque with a touch of deeper pink color remaining.) Arrange on serving platter. Garnish with lemon or lime slices or tarragon sprigs. Pass around remaining tarragon mayonnaise. Serves 6.

PARADISE RANCH INN
7000 Monument Drive
Grants Pass, Oregon
97526
(503) 479-4333

All major credit cards
Expensive

This elegant ranch is the ultimate in country comfort. Guests will enjoy the heated swimming pool, lighted tennis courts and fishing ponds or—if they wish to get a taste of life on the ranch—a few hours of doing the chores.

J E N N Y   L A K E   L O D G E

Chilled Poached Salmon
with Mayonnaise Sauce

1 cup white wine
4 cups water
1 leek, trimmed, cleaned
    and chopped
2 carrots, peeled and
    chopped into
    large chunks
4 stalks celery, cleaned
    and chopped
12 parsley stems
3 bay leaves
12 whole black
    peppercorns
1 lemon, sliced
pinch of salt

five 6-ounce salmon
    fillets, skinned and
    boned
3 ounces German
    cucumber salad
    (see following recipe)
5 leaves Boston lettuce
mayonnaise (see second
    recipe following)
5 hard-boiled eggs
5 lemon slices,
    dusted with paprika
5 parsley sprigs
5 lemon wedges
5 radish roses

In a pot large enough to contain the 5 pieces of salmon in one layer, combine the wine, water, leek, carrots, celery, parsley, bay leaves, peppercorns, lemon and salt to make a court bouillon (a fish-poaching medium). Bring to a simmer and cook for 15 minutes. Immerse the salmon fillets in a single layer in the court bouillon, skin side down, and cover with foil. Simmer (do not boil) for approximately 10 minutes, or until salmon is firm. Take care not to overcook.

When salmon is cooked, place the entire pot on a bed of ice and refrigerate. The salmon and court bouillon must cool together. To serve, place 3 ounces of German cucumber salad (see following recipe) on a leaf of Boston lettuce. Surround a small glass ramekin of mayonnaise (see second recipe following) with a hard-boiled egg cut in 6 slices. Carefully remove the dark brown matter (medial line or nerve), then place one fillet—skin side down—on each of 5 plates. Place a paprika-dusted lemon slice on the salmon. Garnish with a parsley spring, lemon wedge and radish rose. Serves 5.

JENNY LAKE LODGE

German Cucumber Salad:

3 cucumbers
¼ cup salt
1 cup sour cream
juice of 1 lemon
pinch of white pepper

dash of Worcestershire Sauce
2 green onions, minced (optional)

Peel cucumbers and cut lengthwise. Remove the seeds. Cut into ¼" slices. Place in a colander and sprinkle with salt. Allow to drain for 2 hours. Whip sour cream with lemon juice, white pepper and Worcestershire Sauce and green onions, if desired. Blend quickly with cucumber. Season to taste and chill.

Mayonnaise:

3 egg yolks
juice of 1 lemon
2 pinches of dry mustard

pinch of white pepper
1 pint of salad oil
pinch of salt (optional)

Place yolks, lemon juice, mustard and white pepper in a mixing bowl and beat well. (An electric mixer can be used.) Whisk or mix in salad oil very slowly in a thin, steady stream, beating vigorously and constantly. Adjust seasoning if desired.

JENNY LAKE LODGE
P.O. Box 240
Moran, Wyoming
83013
(307) 733-4677

MC/V/AE
Very expensive

Guests enjoy horseback riding, bicycling and the beauty of some of the Grand Teton National Park's most outstanding scenery.

*The Victorian Villa
Union City, Michigan*

Sharon Van Loan's
Cold Salmon with Mustard Sauce

5 to 10 pounds cleaned
   whole fresh salmon (For
   fish with head and tail,
   allow about 1 pound
   per person.)
2 tablespoons lemon juice
¾ cup mayonnaise
3 to 4 stalks celery with
   leaves, chopped

3 to 4 onion slices
garnishes of lemon
   wedges, cucumber slices
   and parsley sprigs
mustard sauce (see
   following recipe)

Preheat oven to 450°. Oil a large piece of heavy foil.

Rinse and pat salmon dry. Allow to stand at room temperature for 1½ to 2 hours. Blend lemon juice into mayonnaise. Combine mixture with celery and onion and put into the cavity of the fish. Wrap the fish in the oiled foil, place on a large cookie sheet and bake for 10 to 12 minutes per pound, or until the flesh along the backbone is just beginning to lose its translucence. Turn fish over about halfway through baking time. When done, unwrap foil to release steam and allow salmon to cool. Remove skin from exposed side of fish and gently scrape brown matter (nerve and fat tissue) away. Spoon out mayonnaise stuffing and place fish on serving platter surrounded by stuffing. Decorate with lemon wedges, cucumber slices and lots of parsley. Serve with mustard sauce (see following recipe). Serves 6 to 8.

Island Hotel
Cedar Key, Florida

STEAMBOAT INN

Mustard Sauce

2 egg yolks
2 tablespoons Dijon
    mustard
1½ teaspoons dry
    mustard
1 teaspoon salt
dash of Cayenne pepper
2 teaspoons tarragon
    vinegar

¾ cup vegetable oil
1 tablespoon chopped
    shallots
1 tablespoon sour cream
¼ teaspoon Bovril™
    bouillon, dissolved in 1
    tablespoon warm water
3 tablespoons heavy
    cream

Put yolks, mustards, salt and Cayenne into blender jar and blend until very thick. Blend in vinegar. Slowly add vegetable oil with blender running. When thick and well mixed, add shallots, sour cream, dissolved bouillon and cream. Blend and store in refrigerator until ready to use. (May be made up to several days in advance and kept in the refrigerator.)

This amount is adequate for a small fish. For a 10-pound fish, double the recipe.

STEAMBOAT INN
HC 60, Box 36
Idleyld Park, Oregon
97447
(503) 496-3495

MC/V
Moderate

On the Umpqua River in the Cascade Mountains, this favorite Oregon fishing lodge is famous for its hearty fishermen's dinners.

BED & BREAKFAST HAWAII

Papaya Seed Dressing

1 teaspoon salt
½ cup sugar
1½ teaspoons dry mustard
1 cup red wine vinegar
2 cups salad oil

2 tablespoons papaya
    seeds
½ cup chopped
    macadamia nuts
½ onion, minced

In a blender, mix salt, sugar, mustard and vinegar. Add oil gradually with blender running. Remove to a serving bowl. In blender, blend papaya seeds, macadamia nuts and onion together. Stir into oil and vinegar mixture. Best served chilled over any type of tossed greens. Serves 6 or more.

BED & BREAKFAST
HAWAII
P.O. Box 449
Kapia, Hawaii
96746
(808) 822-1582

No credit cards
Inexpensive to moderate

This is one of Hawaii's two B & B reservation service organizations, which place visitors in private guest houses.

SHELTER HARBOR INN

Creamed Lobster and Johnnycakes

4 tablespoons butter
1 teaspoon finely minced
  shallots
4 tablespoons all-purpose
  flour
1 cup fish stock (or bottled
  clam juice), hot
¼ cup Madeira
1 cup heavy cream
⅛ teaspoon nutmeg

⅛ teaspoon salt
⅛ teaspoon freshly ground
  pepper
⅛ teaspoon Cayenne
  pepper
2 cups lobster meat
  (reserving whole claw
  meat for garnish)
12 johnnycakes (see
  following recipe)

Melt butter in a heavy saucepan. Add shallots and sauté over moderate heat until tender. Stir in flour and cook, stirring constantly for about 2 minutes, without browning. Remove from heat and stir in the hot stock gradually. Return to heat and stir with a wire whisk until smooth and thick. Stir in Madeira and then heavy cream. Season with nutmeg, salt, pepper and Cayenne. Fold in lobster meat (except for reserved claw). Serve creamed lobster over 3 johnnycakes and garnish with claw. Serves 4 to 6.

SHELTER HARBOR INN JOHNNYCAKES:

2 cups white cornmeal
1½ teaspoons salt
2 teaspoons sugar
2 cups boiling water
½ cup milk, scalded and
  still hot

1 egg, lightly beaten
½ cup bacon fat or other
  cooking oil (enough to
  keep griddle greased)

Mix cornmeal, salt and sugar. Add boiling water and milk and mix well. Stir in egg. Drop by tablespoon onto a medium hot, well-greased griddle or heavy frying pan and fry for 5 minutes on each side. Makes 16 to 20 johnnycakes. Serves 4 to 6.

SHELTER HARBOR INN
Post Road
Shelter Harbor
Westerly, Rhode Island
02891
(401) 322-8883

MC/V/AE
Moderate

This 18-room 18th-century farmhouse-turned-B & B inn is noted for its country cooking.

Roast Leg of Venison

leg of deer (weights will
  vary)
salt and pepper to taste
garlic (one or more cloves,
  depending on size of
  roast)

2 pounds sliced bacon
  (adjust quantity to the
  size of the roast)

Preheat oven to 500°.

Strip all fat from leg of deer. Rub well with salt and pepper. Place slivers of garlic in each end of the leg and in the center along the bone. Place in an open roaster. Cover top of the leg completely with strips of bacon. Put meat thermometer into the center of the leg, not touching bone. Place roaster in the oven. After 30 minutes at 500°, reduce heat to 300°. Cook for about 20 minutes per pound or until desired doneness is reached. (Internal temperature for medium rare will be 150°.) Slice and serve hot. Sliced, cooked onions make an excellent side dish. Serves 2 to 6, depending on the size of the roast.

Wild Ducks with Chestnut Stuffing

4 wild ducks
3½ cups shelled chestnuts
2 cups seedless raisins
¼ cup butter
1 teaspoon salt
dash of pepper
½ cup heavy cream

1 cup bread crumbs
2 minced onions,
  or to taste
4 stalks celery, minced,
  or to taste
½ cup heavy cream

Preheat oven to 350°.

Clean ducks and soak in cold, clear water or in a little soda water for one hour. Wash and drain.

Prepare the stuffing by boiling the chestnuts in water until soft. Cook raisins in a little water, and drain. Drain chestnuts, and put them through a potato ricer or sieve. Add remaining ingredients with enough heavy cream to bind stuffing and mix well.

Stuff ducks with dressing and place them in a roasting pan. Roast for about 1½ hours. During the last 30 minutes of roasting, add ½ cup heavy cream to the pan. Serve with pan juices ladled over duck. Serve one duck per person.

THE MANSION
7 Rice Avenue
Bayfield, Wisconsin
54814
(715) 779-5408

No credit cards
Moderate

The Mansion, an historic 4-room inn skirting Lake Superior in northern Wisconsin, serves exquisite Edwardian luncheons.

PATCHWORK QUILT COUNTRY INN, INC.

Buttermilk Pecan Chicken

¾ cup (1½ sticks) butter
1 cup buttermilk
1 egg, lightly beaten
1 cup all-purpose flour
1 cup ground pecans
¼ cup sesame seeds

1 tablespoon paprika
1 tablespoon salt
⅛ teaspoon pepper
2 to 3½ pounds broiler-
  fryers, cut up
½ cup pecan halves

Preheat oven to 350°. Place butter in large shallow roasting pan and melt in oven. Remove and set aside.

In shallow dish mix buttermilk and egg. In medium bowl combine flour, ground pecans, sesame seeds, paprika, salt and pepper. Coat chicken in buttermilk mixture, then in flour mixture. Place in roasting pan, turning to coat all sides with butter, finishing with skin side up. Scatter pecan halves over chicken and bake about 1½ to 1¾ hours, until chicken is deep golden brown. Serves 8.

PATCHWORK QUILT
COUNTRY INN
11748 C.R. #2
Middlebury, Indiana
46540
(219) 825-2417

No credit cards
Moderate

Located in the heart of Amish country, this Hoosier country inn lives up to its name with patchwork quilts on all the beds.

THE LONE MOUNTAIN RANCH

Dill Bread

2 tablespoons active
  dry yeast
½ cup lukewarm water
4 tablespoons minced
  fresh dill weed
2 tablespoons butter
2 cups cottage cheese

4 tablespoons brown sugar
2 tablespoons minced
  onion
2 teaspoons salt
½ teaspoon baking soda
2 eggs
4½ cups all-purpose flour

Combine yeast and lukewarm water and set aside. Mix together dill and butter. Combine the remaining ingredients to form dough. After the yeast has begun to bubble, work it into the dough, along with the dill butter. Mix in cottage cheese, brown sugar, onion, salt and baking soda mixture. Knead in flour. Knead for 5 minutes or until gluten forms. The dough should be sticky. Allow it to rise until double in size. Punch down. Allow to rise again until double in size. Preheat oven to 350°. Punch down dough and roll into 2 loaves. Bake for about 45 minutes until golden brown. When done, bread will sound hollow when bottom of pan is thumped. Loaves each yield 16 slices.

LONE MOUNTAIN
RANCH
Box 145
Big Sky, Montana
59716
(406) 995-4644

MC/V/AE
Expensive

These log cabins near Yellowstone National Park are a family favorite for a summer ranch experience or winter ski vacation.

Filet of Salmon Noilly

butter	½ cup Noilly Prat
6 medium shallots, minced	½ cup water
4 fillets of salmon,	2 tablespoons lemon juice
approximately ¾	4 large white
pound each	mushroom caps
salt and pepper	8 small potatoes, boiled
2 cups dry white wine	1 small can salmon caviar
1 cup heavy cream	4 fleurons
small bouquet garni	parsley

Preheat oven to 400°. Butter flat rectangular baking dish.

Spread shallots on bottom of dish. Arrange salmon fillets on top and season with salt and pepper. Pour wine and half of cream over salmon, and add bouquet garni. Bake for 20 minutes, or until salmon is somewhat firm to the touch. Remove fillets from dish and keep warm.

Pour cooking juice into saucepan and bring rest of the cream to a boil. Reduce to ⅔ original volume (about 5 minutes). Whisk in Noilly Prat and boil for 2 minutes longer. Whisk sauce to control cooking and to emulsify.

Bring water and lemon juice, with a pinch of salt added, to a boil. Flute mushroom caps with knife and parboil for 5 minutes. Remove from heat and keep warm.

Place salmon fillets on center of a platter. Cover with sauce. On each fillet put one teaspoon salmon caviar and one mushroom cap. Arrange potatoes and fleurons around edge of platter and garnish with parsley. Serves 4.

INN AT PHILLIPS MILL
North River Road
New Hope, Pennsylvania
18938
Dining: (215) 862-9919
Lodging: (215) 862-2984

No credit cards
Expensive

Guests at this 5-bedroom stone barn will delight in candlelit dinners and the French cuisine which has made this establishment a favorite.

The Webber Place
Yountville, California

Sour Cream Crescent Rolls

½ cup butter
1 cup sour cream
¼ cup sugar
1 teaspoon salt
3 tablespoons active dry
   yeast

¼ cup lukewarm water
2 eggs, lightly beaten
5 to 6 cups flour
½ cup melted butter

Preheat oven to 250°.

Dissolve yeast in warm water and set aside. Melt butter in saucepan until it bubbles. Remove from heat and set aside. In a large bowl, combine sour cream, sugar and salt. Stir butter into sour cream mixture and heat to lukewarm. Stir into yeast and add eggs. Work in flour. Dough should be somewhat sticky. Cover with plastic and refrigerate 2 to 4 hours. Divide dough into 4 balls. Roll one ball out into a circle, brush with melted butter and cut into 12 sections (like a pizza). Roll sections from wide to narrow tip and curve slightly to form crescents. Place on greased baking sheet. Repeat with remaining balls of dough. Allow to rise one hour. Bake at 350° for 20 minutes. Serves 8.

THE HOME RANCH
Box 822 K
Clark, Colorado
80428
(303) 879-1780

No credit cards
Very expensive

Located near Steamboat Springs, this ranch caters to cross-country skiers in winter and outdoor enthusiasts in other seasons with horseback riding, hiking and fishing on the Elk River.

Kraft's Kountry Kitchen
Dahlonega, Georgia

*The Inn
Manchester, Vermont*

THE VENICE BEACH HOUSE

Elaine's Apple Dumplings

2 cups all-purpose flour
1 teaspoon salt
2 teaspoons baking
 powder
12 tablespoons (1½ sticks)
 chilled butter
½ cup milk
2 cups sugar
2 cups water
¼ teaspoon cinnamon
¼ teaspoon nutmeg
4 tablespoons butter

6 or 8 small apples, cored
 but not skinned
½ cup brown sugar
½ cup raisins and
 chopped nuts,
 combined
½ cup granola
1 teaspoon cinnamon
2 teaspoons butter
1 cup or more sour cream,
 to taste

To prepare the pastry, sift together flour, salt and baking powder. Cut in the chilled butter, add milk and stir just long enough to moisten the flour. Roll dough out on floured board to ¼" thickness and allow to rest for at least ½ hour.

Meanwhile, prepare a syrup of the sugar, water and spices. Simmer for 5 minutes, then add 4 tablespoons butter. Set aside.

Preheat oven to 275°. Butter a jelly roll pan.

Peel and partially core apples, to create a cavity, but do not cut through bottom. Cut pastry into 5" squares (depending on size of apple), and place one apple on each square. Fill the cavity with a mixture of brown sugar, raisins, nuts and cinnamon, and dot with ½ teaspoon butter. Fold corners and pinch all edges together. Repeat with remaining apples. Place one inch apart on the jelly roll pan. Pour syrup over the "dumplings." Bake for 35 minutes. Serve with sour cream. Serves 6 to 8.

THE VENICE
BEACH HOUSE
15 30th Avenue
Venice, California
90291
(213) 823-1966

MC/V/AE
Expensive

An 8-room historic land-mark, The Venice Beach House is not far from the beach and other attractions of this unusual Los Angeles community.

GARRATT MANSION

Herbal Popovers

3 eggs
1 cup milk
1 cup all-purpose flour
3 tablespoons butter,
  melted

1 teaspoon dried thyme,
  sage or crushed basil
½ teaspoon celery salt

Preheat oven to 450°. Butter eight 6-ounce custard cups.

In blender container, mix eggs, milk, flour, butter, herbs and celery salt. Cover and process at low speed until just smooth. Spoon about ⅓ cup of the batter into each custard cup. Bake for 15 minutes. Reduce heat to 375° and bake for 30 minutes longer or until browned. Serve immediately. Serves 4.

GARRATT MANSION
900 Union Street
Alameda, California
94501
(415) 521-4779

No credit cards
Moderate

In this quiet San Francisco island suburb, guests can bicycle to the beach, observe the harbor life, or stroll down Alameda's shady streets.

MOUNT VIEW HOTEL

Orville Knight's Oyster Stew

4 tablespoons butter
1 tablespoon chopped
  shallots
liquid from oysters
  plus enough clam juice
  to make one quart
2 cups cream
salt and pepper to taste
¼ teaspoon Tabasco
2 tablespoons chopped
  green onions

1 tablespoon chopped red
  pepper (below)
18 oysters, shucked
2 tablespoons grated dry
  cheddar cheese
1 teaspoon grated
  Parmesan
½ teaspoon black caviar
  for garnish

Melt butter in a sauté pan and sauté shallots until they become transparent. Add oyster liquid and clam juice and, over high heat, reduce by ⅔, whisking to prevent over-boiling. Add cream and, continuing to whisk over high heat, reduce by ½. Reduce heat and season with salt, pepper and Tabasco. Add green onion and red pepper. Return sauce to a simmer and add oysters. Cook for 5 minutes, taking care not to overcook. Add cheddar cheese and place in an oven-proof soup terrine. Sprinkle with Parmesan cheese and place under broiler, just long enough to brown. Garnish with caviar. Serves 6.

MOUNT VIEW HOTEL
1457 Lincoln
Calistoga, California
94515
(707) 942-6877

No credit cards
Moderate to expensive

This elaborate 34-room Art Deco inn is located in a popular spa resort at the northern end of the Napa Valley.

The Lyme Inn
Lyme, New Hampshire

THE GRISWOLD INN

Monte Carlo Sandwiches

8 ounces sliced turkey
12 slices white bread,
    thickly buttered (use
    softened butter)
8 ounces sliced ham

4 ounces sliced Swiss
    cheese
8 eggs, lightly beaten
6 ounces butter

Preheat oven to 350°.

Place ¼ of the sliced turkey on top of one slice of buttered bread. On another slice, put ¼ of the sliced ham and ¼ of the sliced Swiss cheese. Stack the ham and cheese layer on top of the turkey layer. Place the last slice of bread on top (bread will be on the top, in the middle and on the bottom). Repeat with remaining bread, meats and cheese. Cut crust off and cut in half. Wrap sandwiches in plastic wrap and refrigerate until butter has hardened. Dip sandwiches into beaten egg. Melt some butter in a sauté pan and sauté sandwiches a few at a time until browned on both sides. Place in oven and bake for 10 minutes. Serves 4.

GRISWOLD INN
Essex, Connecticut
06426
(203) 767-0991

MC/V/AE/DC
Expensive

Located in a riverside town, the Griswold Inn has been in operation for 207 years.

L O W E L L   I N N

Red Cabbage

1 medium-size head of red cabbage	1½ cups water
1 medium-size onion	1 cup cider vinegar
2 large cooking apples (approximately 1 pound)	½ cup sugar
	1 teaspoon salt
1 tablespoon bacon fat or butter	1 bay leaf
	2 whole allspice
	6 peppercorns
	1 tablespoon cornstarch

Wash cabbage and remove outer leaves. Quarter cabbage, core and slice. (You should have about 3 quarts.) Slice onion. Pare apples and cut into sixths, removing cores. Toss cabbage, onion and apples together in bacon fat (or butter) which has been melted in a Dutch oven. Add water, cider vinegar, sugar, salt and spices. Simmer uncovered for 20 minutes or until desired tenderness is obtained. Combine cornstarch with a little cold water to make a paste. Add hot cabbage and stir constantly until thickened (about one minute). Makes 8 servings.

LOWELL INN
102 North Second Street
Stillwater, Minnesota
55082
(612) 439-1100

MC/V/AE/DC
Expensive to very
expensive

This rural retreat is located in historic Stillwater, near the bluff of the St. Croix River and not too far from St. Paul.

Society Hill Hotel
Philadelphia, Pennsylvania

*Lowell Inn
Stillwater, Minnesota*

DIE HEIMAT COUNTRY INN

Sauerkraut

2 medium-size heads of
   cabbage

1 teaspoon sugar
2 tablespoons salt

Mix all ingredients thoroughly in a large bowl. Mash cabbage with potato masher until juice collects. Cover bowl with cloth, and let stand for 2 hours. Press kraut into 3 sterilized quart jars as firmly as possible, then fill with the liquid collected in bowl. Fit screw tops loosely so that the kraut can ferment. Let stand at room temperature for several days. Press down again, and if necessary, make a weak salt solution (about 1½ cups salt to one quart water) to fill jars with liquid. Screw tops on tightly and store in a cool place. Sauerkraut is ready to use in 4 weeks. It may be eaten raw as a relish, just as it comes from the jar, or cooked.

Plain Cooked Sauerkraut

2 cups sauerkraut
2 tablespoons lard

caraway seed (optional)
water to cover

Cook all together for 15 minutes and serve.

Cooked Sauerkraut and Potato

2 cups cooked
   sauerkraut

1 medium raw potato,
   grated

Add potato to sauerkraut, cook 10 minutes, and serve.

DIE HEIMAT
COUNTRY INN
Homestead, Iowa 52236
(319) 622-3937

MC/V
Inexpensive

This century-old, 19-room inn is in the middle of Iowa's historic Amana colonies.

Chateau Madeleine
LaPointe, Wisconsin

L O G W O O D   I N N

Anadama Bread

According to legend, this delicious bread was invented by an early American fisherman whose wife did not bake. He named his creation after her: Anna, damn her.

7½ to 8½ cups unsifted
* all-purpose flour*
2¾ teaspoon salt
2 packages active dry
* yeast*

½ cup butter, softened
2¾ cups warm water
* (130°F)*
¾ cup molasses
1¼ cups cornmeal

Combine about 2½ cups flour with salt and yeast. Stir in softened butter. Add water and molasses slowly, blending well. Beat at medium speed with an electric mixer for two minutes. Stir in ½ cup flour, and beat at high speed for 2 minutes more. Stir in cornmeal and enough additional flour to form a stiff dough. Turn out onto a floured board and knead until smooth and elastic (about 10 minutes). Place in a large buttered bowl, and butter the top of the dough. Cover and allow it to rise in a warm place until double in bulk (about one hour). Punch down and divide into two parts. Shape dough into 14" by 9" rectangles. Roll the dough up from its short upper end, and seal the sides, folding the sealed ends over and pressing them closed. Place loaves with seam side down in two buttered loaf pans. Cover with a towel, and allow them to rise until double in bulk (about 45 minutes). Bake in a preheated oven set at 375° for 40 to 45 minutes or until the loaves sound hollow when tapped. Remove from the pans, and cool on a wire rack. Loaves freeze well.

Aunt Margaret's
Pennsylvania Dutch Sticky Buns

1 package active dry yeast	⅓ cup sugar
2 cups warm water (130°F)	1 stick (4 ounces) butter, softened
2 tablespoons sugar	1 cup butter, softened
5½ to 6 cups all-purpose flour	2 tablespoons sugar
1 egg, beaten	1 teaspoon cinnamon
1 teaspoon salt	1½ cup syrup of choice
	1 cup walnuts

In a large bowl, dissolve yeast in the warm water and stir until dissolved. Add sugar and two cups flour. Beat until smooth. Allow this mixture to stand for 15 to 20 minutes. With a spoon, add the egg, salt, sugar, and 4 ounces softened butter. Gradually mix in the remaining flour. Cover with a towel, and allow dough to rise for 1 to 1½ hours in a warm spot. Roll out the dough on a floured board until it is a 15" by 24" rectangle. Spread it with 1 cup softened butter, and sprinkle sugar and cinnamon over the top. Roll the dough rectangle lengthwise, and slice it into one-inch slices. Place slices side-by-side into pans which have been buttered and lined with syrup and walnuts. Allow buns to rise another hour. Bake in preheated 400° oven until nicely browned. Makes 12 to 15 buns.

LOGWOOD INN & CHALETS
Box 2290, Route 1
Stowe, Vermont
05672
(802) 253-7354

MC/V/AE
Moderate

Located beside a mountain stream, this quiet, peaceful establishment is a year-round getaway, with swimming pool and tennis courts, and Stowe's famed ski slopes nearby.

Sour Cream Walnut Pie

1 tablespoon butter	2 cups walnuts
⅔ cup brown sugar	2 teaspoons vanilla
1 cup light corn syrup	¼ teaspoon salt
2 eggs, lightly beaten	1 pie crust fitted into a pie tin
1⅔ cups sour cream	

Preheat oven to 350°.

In a saucepan, heat butter, brown sugar, and corn syrup until all ingredients have liquified. Remove from heat. Combine eggs, sour cream, walnuts, vanilla, and salt, and stir into the heated mixture. Return saucepan to stove and cook for 5 more minutes on low heat, stirring constantly to prevent the sour cream and eggs from coagulating. Pour into pie crust and bake for one hour. Serves 8.

STAFFORD'S BAY
VIEW INN
P.O. Box 3
Petoskey, Michigan 49770
(616) 347-2771

MC/V/AE
Expensive

Located on Little Traverse Bay on the upper reaches of Lake Michigan, this inn is a Michigan historic site.

GREENVILLE ARMS

Moravian Orange Rolls

5 to 6 cups unsifted
　　all-purpose flour
⅔ cup sugar
1 teaspoon salt
2 packages active
　　dry yeast
⅓ cup softened butter
1 cup warm water (120° to
　　130°F)
1 cup mashed potatoes at
　　room temperature

2 eggs at room
　　temperature
½ cup softened butter
2 cups firmly packed light
　　brown sugar
2 tablespoons orange juice
1 teaspoon ground
　　cinnamon
1 teaspoon grated orange
　　peel

In a large bowl, thoroughly mix 1½ cups flour, sugar, salt and yeast. Stir in ⅓ cup softened butter. Gradually add warm water and beat 2 minutes with an electric mixer at medium speed. Add potatoes, eggs and ½ cup flour. Beat well. Stir in enough additional flour to make a soft dough. Turn out onto lightly-floured board. Knead for 8 to 10 minutes. Place in a greased bowl, turning to grease the top. Cover and allow dough to rise in a warm, draft-free place until doubled in bulk (about one hour).

Meanwhile, cream ½ cup butter with brown sugar. Blend in orange juice, cinnamon and orange peel. When doubled, punch down dough. Turn out onto lightly-floured board and divide in half. Roll half of the dough into a 12" by 18" rectangle. Spread with half the sugar mixture and roll up like a jelly roll. Seal edges firmly. Slice into 18 equal pieces. Repeat with remaining dough and sugar mixture. Arrange on edge in four staggered rows of nine slices in a buttered 9" pan. Allow rolls to rise about one hour until they have doubled in size.

Bake at 350° about 30 minutes or until done. Cool on wire racks. Yields 36 rolls.

GREENVILLE ARMS
Greenville, New York
12083
(518) 966-5219

No credit cards
Expensive

The former home of William Vanderbilt in the foothills of the Catskills, the Greenville Arms offers 7 acres of lush lawn, a quaint stream and bridges, gardens and swimming pools for a relaxing week-end getaway.

E D W A R D I A N   I N N

Edwardian Buns

5 to 6 cups all-purpose
   flour
1 cup sugar
2 packages active dry
   yeast
1 teaspoon salt
¾ cup water

½ cup butter
2 eggs
½ cup cooked mashed
   potatoes
⅛ teaspoon ground
   nutmeg
melted butter

Combine one cup flour, sugar, yeast and salt in a large mixing bowl. Stir well. Heat water and butter in a small saucepan (temperature should reach 115° to 120°). Gradually add hot mixture to flour mixture, beating at low speed with an electric mixer until combined. Beat 2 minutes more at medium speed. Beat in eggs, potato, nutmeg and ¾ cup flour and continue beating for an additional 2 minutes. Gradually stir in enough of the remaining flour to make a soft dough. Turn dough out onto a well-floured surface and knead until smooth and elastic (about 10 minutes). Shape into a ball and place in a well-buttered bowl, turning the dough to cover with butter. Cover and allow to rise in a warm, draft-free place for 1½ hours. Punch down and let rise once more, until double in bulk. Divide dough into 12 equal parts. Roll each into a ball and place on buttered baking sheet. Press balls lightly with fingertips to shape them into buns. Cover and allow to rise until double. Brush buns with melted butter. Bake at 375° for 15 to 20 minutes or until golden. Remove immediately. Yields 12.

EDWARDIAN INN
317 Biscoe
Helena, Arkansas
72342
(501) 338-9155

MC/V/AE
Moderate

This antique-appointed 12-room inn evokes the feeling of life in a Mississippi River town at the turn of the century.

The Swag
Waynesville, North Carolina

THE VOSS INN B & B

Sticky Buns

½ cup sugar
6 cups unsifted all-purpose
  flour
1½ teaspoons salt
2 packages active dry yeast
1 cup milk
⅔ cup water
¼ cup butter
2 eggs, at room
  temperature

¾ cup melted butter
  (approximately)
½ cup brown sugar
  (approximately)
⅓ teaspoon cinnamon
  (approximately)
¼ cup white sugar
  (approximately)
¼ cup peanut oil
  (approximately)

Spray 4 round cake pans with Pam vegetable cooking spray. Mix 5 cups flour, sugar, salt and yeast. Heat to lukewarm the milk, water and ¼ cup butter, and mix them into the flour mixture. Add eggs, working into a dough with your hands (or use the dough hook of an electric mixer). Slowly add last cup of flour. Turn onto a board and knead for 10 minutes. Allow dough to rise in a greased bowl for 20 to 30 minutes. Punch down on a lightly-floured board and roll into a rectangle. Melt the remaining butter. Using a little more than half of the melted butter, cover the bottoms of the 4 round cake pans. Pour the rest of the butter over the dough rectangle, spreading to cover. Sprinkle brown sugar over butter in pans and over the dough rectangle. Combine cinnamon and white sugar and sprinkle over the dough, roll it up, and slice into 24 buns. Place 6 buns in each pan and brush tops with peanut oil. Refrigerate, covered, for 2 to 24 hours.

Preheat oven to 375°. Allow buns to stand at room temperature for 20 to 30 minutes, then bake 25 minutes or until done. Yields 24 sticky buns.

THE VOSS INN
BED & BREAKFAST
319 South Wilson
Bozeman, Montana
59715
(406) 587-0982

MC/V
Moderate

This 100-year-old red brick mansion lies in the heart of the university town of Bozeman. Each of its 6 guest rooms has a restored brass or iron bed and a unique personality.

Romeo Inn
Ashland, Oregon

Beer Bagels

2 tablespoons active dry
    yeast
one 12-ounce can of
    beer, at room
    temperature

3 tablespoons sugar
1 tablespoon salt
4½ cups all-purpose flour
    cornmeal (enough to dust
    a baking sheet)

Dissolve yeast in ½ cup lukewarm beer. Combine remaining beer with sugar and salt. Stir until sugar is dissolved, then add one cup flour and yeast mixture. Stir in 3½ cups flour to make a stiff dough and knead until smooth (approximately 10 minutes). Cover and let rise in a warm, draft-free place for one hour.

Preheat oven to 375°. Divide dough into 10 pieces and let it relax for 3 minutes. Bring 2 quarts water and one tablespoon sugar to a boil. Reduce heat and let simmer. Shape balls into bagels and allow to rest for 10 minutes. Drop bagels into simmering water, 2 or 3 at a time, for 45 seconds, turning once. Remove from water and drain on towel. Place on nonstick baking sheet sprinkled with cornmeal and bake for 30 minutes. Yields 10 bagels.

ROMEO INN
295 Idaho Street
Ashland, Oregon
97520

No credit cards
Expensive

A large, comfortable guest house with swimming pool, hot tub and afternoon tea, the Romeo Inn is within walking distance of Ashland's Shakespeare Festival Theater.

*Preston House
Santa Fe, New Mexico*

Apple Strudel

4 to 6 cooking apples, sliced	2½ cups bread crumbs
2 tablespoons sugar	(from dark,
1 tablespoon vanilla	"interesting" breads)
grated rind of 1 orange,	2 cups sugar
tangerine or lemon	2 cups chopped walnuts
12 sheets phyllo dough	¼ cup powdered sugar
1½ sticks (12 tablespoons)	1 cup whipped cream
butter, melted	cognac vanilla* to taste

Preheat oven to 350°. Butter a baking dish.

Toss apples with sugar, vanilla and orange rind, and set aside. Place 3 sheets of phyllo dough on a fresh towel and brush with melted butter. Sprinkle heavily with a mixture of one cup each bread crumbs, sugar and walnuts. Place 2 more sheets of phyllo dough onto the first layer and repeat the process. Finally add 2 more sheets of phyllo dough topped with the butter and ½ cup bread crumbs.

Place the apples in a row, front to back, on the far right side of the phyllo. Using the towel to help, roll the dough and apples towards the left. Place on a baking sheet and butter the strudel roll well. Bake for about 25 minutes or until golden in color. Place the baked strudel on a board, and slice into pieces. Sift powdered sugar over the roll. Serve with whipped cream laced with cognac vanilla* and sweetened with powdered sugar. Serves 8.

*Kay Tripp of Eiler's Inn prepares her own vanilla by soaking 10 vanilla beans (sliced and scraped) and seeds in a bottle of "the best quality cognac you are willing to buy." The bottle is turned each day and matures in a couple of weeks. As the contents of the bottle dwindle, the mixture can be extended with more beans and cognac.

EILER'S INN
741 South Coast Highway
Laguna Beach, California
92651
(714) 494-3004

MC/V/AE
Very expensive

This inn, built around a courtyard, serves breakfast and afternoon wine and cheese around a fountain.

The Red Clover Inn
Mendon, Vermont

SUTTER CREEK INN

Apple Oatmeal Crisp

4 cups tart cooking apples,
 peeled and thinly sliced
1½ tablespoons fresh
 lemon juice
3½ tablespoons
 granulated sugar
⅓ cup all-purpose flour

1 cup rolled oats
½ cup firmly packed
 brown sugar
1 teaspoon cinnamon
1 cup chopped walnuts
½ teaspoon salt
½ cup melted butter

Preheat oven to 375°. Generously butter a 9" square pan.

Combine apples, lemon juice and granulated sugar and put in pan. In a bowl combine flour, oats, brown sugar, cinnamon, walnuts, salt and melted butter and sprinkle over apples. Bake for 35 minutes.

SUTTER CREEK INN
P.O. Box 385
Sutter Creek, California
95685
(209) 267-5606

No credit cards
Expensive

This classic California inn is in a gold rush town popular for antiquing and sightseeing. The inn features swinging beds which can be stabilized, and fireplaces in almost every room.

FLEMING JONES HOMESTEAD

Homestead Baked Apples

4 apples (Rome, Granny
 Smith or Pippin)
4 to 16 pieces candied fruit
16 to 24 currants
4 teaspoons butter
4 teaspoons frozen orange
 juice concentrate

4 teaspoons ground
 walnuts
4 teaspoons cinnamon
4 teaspoons cloves
4 teaspoons sugar
¼ cup water
cream (optional)

Preheat oven to 350°.

Peel apples ⅔ of the way down. Remove stem and core. Rinse apples and place in baking dish. In the inside of each apple place: 2 to 4 small pieces candied fruit, 4 to 6 currants, one teaspoon butter and one teaspoon orange juice concentrate. Sprinkle some ground walnuts, cinnamon, cloves and sugar over the top of each apple. Add a small amount of water to the bottom of the baking dish (the apples themselves will release quite a bit of juice). Cover and bake for 30 to 35 minutes, or until the outsides begin to puff out, sputter and froth. Place each apple in an individual dish. Spoon juice over apples. Serve either hot or cold. Cream may be served on the side. Baked apples may be prepared in advance and reheated. Serves 4.

THE FLEMING JONES
HOMESTEAD
3170 Newton Road
Placerville, California
95667
(916) 626-5840

No credit cards
Moderate

Located in the heart of the gold rush country, The Fleming Jones Homestead is a century-old farmhouse, complete with burros, chickens, ducks and a pony.

STONE HEDGE INN

Southern Pecan Pie

two 10" pastry-lined
  pie shells
7 eggs
1 quart Karo dark corn
  syrup

1 cup dark brown sugar
4 ounces (1 stick) butter
1 teaspoon salt
3 cups pecans

Preheat oven to 400°.

Pre-bake pastry shells for 10 minutes. Mix together all ingredients except pecans. Fill each shell with 1½ cups of pecans. Pour filling over pecans and bake 40 minutes or until done. Makes 2 pies, each of which serves 6 to 8.

STONE HEDGE INN
Box 366
Tryon, North Carolina
28782
(704) 859-9114

MC/V
Moderate to expensive

Poised in a beautiful mountain setting on the North-South Carolina border, Stone Hedge Inn has 4 rooms and a swimming pool, and serves memorable meals.

The Rupley House Inn
Placerville, California

THE FOXES BED & BREAKFAST INN

Rhubarb Pie

1½ cups butter	1 cup sugar
4 cups all-purpose flour	2 tablespoons quick-
1 tablespoon sugar	cooking tapioca
1 teaspoon salt	⅛ teaspoon salt
1 egg	½ cup seedless raisins
1 tablespoon white	(optional)
vinegar	⅛ teaspoon cinnamon
ice water	(optional)
4 cups rhubarb, cut into	
¾" lengths	

To prepare pastry, work butter into flour, sugar and salt to form pea-sized particles. Drop egg into an 8-ounce cup measure. Add white vinegar and enough ice water to fill the cup. Beat liquids together and add to flour/butter mixture, working the liquid into the solids until the dough forms a ball. Knead lightly on a floured board and roll into separate balls the size of oranges. (This recipe yields more than is needed for a single pie. Freeze the leftover balls and have ready for next time.) Allow the dough to rest, covered, in the refrigerator for at least ½ hour before rolling out 2 separate crusts. Fit one into the bottom of a flour-dusted pie plate. Reserve the other for the top crust.

Preheat oven to 450°.

To prepare the pie filling, combine rhubarb, sugar, tapioca and salt. Fill the pie shell with rhubarb mixture. Cut a design for steam vents into the top crust. Brush edge of lower crust with cold water. Place top crust over the pie, and press the edges of both crusts together to seal. Trim excess dough. Flute the rim. Bake for 15 minutes, then reduce heat to 325°, and continue baking for an additional 30 minutes or until the rhubarb is tender. For variety, add seedless raisins and/or a bit of cinnamon to the filling. Yields one pie serving 6 to 8.

THE FOXES BED & BREAKFAST INN
77 Main Street
P.O. Box 159
Sutter Creek, California 95685
(209) 267-5882

AE
Expensive to very expensive

In the heart of California's gold rush country, this inn delivers a bountiful breakfast to each of its 3 elegant antique-appointed suites: Honeymoon, Anniversary and Imperial.

CHATEAU MADELEINE

Chocolate Sour Cream Cake

4 ounces unsweetened
   baking chocolate
¾ cup milk
1 cup firmly packed light
   brown sugar
3 egg yolks
2 cups cake flour
1 teaspoon baking soda
½ teaspoon salt
½ cup softened butter
1 cup granulated sugar

¼ cup water
¼ cup sour cream
1 teaspoon vanilla
2 egg whites, stiffly beaten
   yet still moist
3 ounces unsweetened
   chocolate
3 ounces cream cheese
¼ cup milk
4 cups confectioners' sugar

All ingredients should be at room temperature.

Preheat oven to 350°. Butter and flour two 9" cake pans.

In a double boiler, stir together and melt 4 ounces of chocolate, ½ cup of the milk, brown sugar and one egg yolk, stirring occasionally. Set this mixture aside to cool slightly. Before measuring, sift the cake flour. Resift with the baking soda and salt. Cream butter and add the granulated sugar, beating until light. Beat in the last 2 yolks one at a time. Blend together water, ¼ cup of the milk, sour cream and vanilla. Add flour mixture to the butter mixture, in 3 parts, alternately with the liquid ingredients. Stir batter until smooth, then blend in the chocolate which was set aside. Fold in the 2 beaten egg whites. Bake for 25 minutes or until cake sides pull away from the edge of the pan.

Prepare icing by melting the 3 ounces of chocolate in a double boiler. Set aside to cool slightly. Soften the cream cheese in the quarter cup of milk. Gradually add the confectioners' sugar and melted chocolate. Beat until smooth. Assemble and ice the cake in 2 layers.

CHATEAU MADELEINE
P.O. Box 27
LaPointe, Wisconsin
54850
(715) 747-2463

All major credit cards
Moderate

A ferry ride takes guests back in time to a Lake Superior island retreat, where fish fries, sing-alongs, canoeing, and sailing are a few of the favorite activities.

THE OLD COUNTY JAIL

Buttermilk Pie

1½ cups sugar
6 tablespoons butter,
  softened
2 eggs, separated
3 tablespoons all-purpose
  flour
¼ teaspoon ground cloves
1 teaspoon cinnamon
½ teaspoon nutmeg

1½ cups buttermilk
2 teaspoons lemon juice
1 teaspoon grated lemon
  peel
one 9" pie crust, partially
  baked and cooled
1 tablespoon powdered
  sugar

Preheat oven to 350°.

Cream sugar and butter until light. Add egg yolks one at a time, beating well in between. Combine flour and all spices. Beat this into butter mixture. Continue beating, adding in buttermilk in a thin stream. Add lemon juice and rind, stirring constantly. In separate glass bowl, whip egg whites until they come to a peak. Fold gently into batter. Pour mixture into partially-baked pie crust and bake until the pie is set—about 40 minutes. Sprinkle sifted powdered sugar over the top. Serve chilled. Yields one pie which serves 6.

THE OLD COUNTY JAIL
State Highway 4
P.O. Box 157
Washington, Arkansas
71862
(501) 983-2178

MC/V
Moderate

Located in a town that was once the Confederate capital of Arkansas and is now a state historic park, this 6-room inn was built as a jail in 1872 and was the birthplace of the Bowie knife.

The Historic Fairfield Inn
Fairfield, Pennsylvania

Ottauqueechee River Mud Pie

This is the best-selling dessert at The Village Inn.

¼ cup melted butter
1 cup finely-chopped
  fudge chip cookies (or
  other favorite cookies)

½ gallon coffee ice cream
fudge sauce (see following
  recipe)
2 to 3 cups whipped cream

Remove ice cream from freezer to let soften. In a bowl, pour melted butter over cookie crumbs and stir until well blended. In a 9" pie tin, form a crust with the cookie crumb mixture, using your hands or the back of a large spoon. Start with the sides of the pie pan and then press down the bottom. Tamp down the crumbs gently but firmly to keep them in place.

Scoop the softened ice cream into the crust with a large spoon. (The ice cream can start to melt quickly, so work fast or put the ice cream back in the freezer for a few minutes to re-harden.) Gently push the ice cream down to eliminate air pockets. Then smooth around the pie with a cake spatula or knife. Place the pie in the freezer to harden for one hour. Top with your favorite fudge sauce and fresh whipped cream. Serves 8 to 10.

THE VILLAGE INN OF WOODSTOCK
41 Pleasant Street
Woodstock, Vermont 05091
(802) 457-1255

MC/V
Moderate

This antique-appointed Victorian mansion still contains many of its original furnishings.

The Squire's Fudge Sauce

¼ pound butter
5 ounces unsweetened
  baking chocolate

1 pound powdered sugar
1 can evaporated milk
1 teaspoon vanilla

Melt together butter and chocolate in double boiler. Add alternately powdered sugar and evaporated milk. Heat over low burner until sauce bubbles and thickens. Add vanilla. Serve over homemade ice cream or mud pie. Makes 3 to 4 cups, which will serve 10 to 12.

THE SQUIRE TARBOX INN

Pumpkin-Apple Cake

½ cup butter
1½ cups sugar
2 eggs
2 apples, pared, cored
   and grated
1 cup mashed pumpkin
2 cups all-purpose flour
1 teaspoon baking powder

½ teaspoon baking soda
¼ teaspoon salt
½ teaspoon cinnamon
½ teaspoon nutmeg
¼ teaspoon ground cloves
¼ teaspoon ginger
2 tablespoons powdered
   sugar, or to taste

Preheat oven to 350°. Generously butter a tube or bundt pan and dust lightly with flour.

Cream together butter and sugar with electric mixer. Add eggs one at a time, beating well after each addition. Stir in grated apples and mashed pumpkin. Sift together flour, baking powder, baking soda, salt, cinnamon, nutmeg, ground cloves and ginger. Add to pumpkin mixture, stirring well. Pour into pan and bake for 55 minutes. Cool in pan 10 minutes before turning out cake to cool on a wire rack. When cool, sift powdered sugar over top. Makes one cake which serves 8 to 10.

SQUIRE TARBOX INN
RD 2, Box 2160
Wiscasset, Maine
04578
(207) 882-7693

No credit cards
Expensive

At the Squire Tarbox, simple pleasures are memorable—picking raspberries, a peaceful stroll down a pine-needled path, a piece of homemade cheese enjoyed by the fireplace or a conversation with a new-found friend.

THE LYME INN

Indian Pudding

2 eggs, lightly beaten
1 cup cornmeal
½ cup all-purpose flour
½ cup molasses
1 teaspoon salt
½ teaspoon ginger

½ teaspoon cinnamon
2 quarts scalded milk
ice cream or whipped
   cream, according to
   preference

Preheat oven to 350°. Butter a baking dish.

On the top of the stove over medium heat, combine all ingredients except the milk and beat thoroughly. Slowly add milk, stirring constantly, until the mixture thickens. Pour into baking dish and bake for 30 minutes. This keeps well in the refrigerator and can be easily heated in a double boiler. Serve warm with ice cream or whipped cream.

THE LYME INN
Route 10
Lyme, New Hampshire
03768
(603) 795-2222

MC/V/AE
Expensive

This antique-appointed country inn is in a tiny New Hampshire town near the Vermont border.

SPRING BANK FARM INN

Hot Pear Compote

This farm boasts apple, chestnut, walnut and hickory trees. The most bountiful yield, however, comes from 3 aged pear trees whose boughs are heavy with fruit in September and October. These pear recipes are excellent choices for a cool autumn breakfast.

2 cups water
2 tablespoons lemon juice
2 tablespoons sugar

1 teaspoon cinnamon
8 large pears
dash of cinnamon

In a saucepan, bring water, lemon juice, sugar and 1 teaspoon cinnamon to a boil. Peel and halve the pears. Slice into ¼" pieces. Add pear pieces to boiling syrup. Reduce to medium heat and cook until pears soften (about 10 minutes). Serve immediately, topped with a dash of cinnamon. Serves 4.

Pear Butter

2 cups water
2 tablespoons lemon juice
2 tablespoons sugar

1 teaspoon cinnamon
8 large pears

Prepare as for the hot pear compote, but continue to cook until the liquid evaporates and the pears turn to a mash. Refrigerate until ready to use. Spread on toast.

SPRING BANK
FARM INN
7945 Worman's Mill Road
Frederick, Maryland
21701
(301) 694-0440

No credit cards
Expensive

Located in historic Frederick, the Spring Bank Farm Inn is set in rolling countryside near parks for hiking and rural roads for exploring and biking.

Greenville Arms
Greenville, New York

GOSBY HOUSE INN

Bread Pudding

6 eggs
2½ cups half-and-half
½ cup sugar
cinnamon, mace and
    nutmeg, to taste

¼ teaspoon salt
8 day-old croissants
¾ cup currants or raisins

Preheat oven to 350°. Butter a 10" pie plate or quiche dish.

Whisk together eggs, half-and-half, sugar, spices and salt. Pour custard into buttered pan. Break up croissants into bite-sized pieces and spread over custard. Spread currants on top. Press croissants and currants lightly into custard. Bake for about 50 minutes or until it is slightly firm to the touch in the center. Serves 6 to 8.

GOSBY HOUSE INN
643 Light House Avenue
Pacific Grove, California
93950
(408) 375-1287

No credit cards
Very expensive

This elegant 19-room inn is located on the Monterey Peninsula, south of San Francisco, an area of stunning ocean vistas.

WEBBER PLACE

Custard with Berries

3 eggs
⅓ cup brown sugar
½ teaspoon vanilla
2 cups milk, scalded
    and cooled
⅛ teaspoon nutmeg
dash of salt

1 pint fresh berries
½ pint whipped cream,
    slightly sweetened with
    brown sugar
sprinkle of cinnamon
mint sprigs (optional)

Preheat oven to 300°. Butter six 6-ounce custard cups.

Combine eggs, brown sugar and vanilla. Gradually stir in milk. Pour into custard cups and place in 13" by 9" by 2" pan. Pour very hot water into pan to within ½" of tops of cups. Bake about 45 minutes or until knife inserted between center and edge comes out clean. Remove from water and cool.

Spoon fresh berries and slightly whipped cream on top. Add a dash of cinnamon and sprig of mint for garnish. Serves 6.

WEBBER PLACE
6610 Webber Street
Yountville, California
94599
(707) 944-8384

MC/V
Expensive to very expensive

The Webber Place is a village inn featuring antique bathtubs and afternoon tea.

THE GOVERNOR'S INN

Iced Christmas Cherry

3 one-pound cans pitted
    tart cherries (packed in
    water)
2 cinnamon sticks
6 whole cloves
6 whole allspice
1 cup water
½ lemon

½ cup sugar
pinch of salt
1 pint heavy cream
1 tablespoon
    all-purpose flour
2 cups French Medoc wine
sweetened whipped cream
    for garnish

Empty two cans tart cherries and juice into a large pot. Add juice from third can, but reserve cherries. Mix in spices, water, lemon, sugar and pinch of salt. Bring to a boil. In a separate smaller pan, scald cream and whisk in flour. Cool scalded mixture slightly and add to berry mixture. Add wine and bring just to the boiling point. Strain out solids and cool mixture. Add the reserved can of berries and refrigerate. This will keep in the refrigerator for at least 2 weeks.

When ready to serve, place about 5 ounces of chilled potable in a glass bowl or compote—a liner bowl set in crushed ice works well for serving—and garnish with a dollop of whipped cream. Serves 12.

THE GOVERNOR'S INN
86 Main Street
Ludlow, Vermont
05149
(802) 228-8830

MC/V/AE
Expensive

This southern Vermont smalltown B & B is close to 5 lakes, the Black River and Okemo Mountain. Guests sleep soundly in century-old 4-poster brass beds and delight in 4-course gourmet breakfasts.

OAK SQUARE

Old Fashioned Syllabub

Syllabub was served in colonial days as ice cream is now, and is frequently found in cookbooks of the early 18th century.

1½ cups milk
3 eggs
¾ cup sugar

½ teaspoon salt
3 cups light cream
2 cups sweet wine

Scald milk. Beat eggs and add sugar and salt. Gradually mix hot milk into egg mixture and cook over hot water, stirring constantly, until mixture thickens. Cool. Add the light cream and wine and refrigerate. Serve cold in custard cups or glasses. Makes enough for 4 to 6 servings.

OAK SQUARE
1207 Church Street
Port Gibson, Mississippi
39150
(601) 437-4350

MC/V/AE
Expensive

Listed on the National Register of Historic Places, Oak Square is a palatial mansion in a town said by General U.S. Grant to be too beautiful to burn.

A N N I E ' S   B E D   &   B R E A K F A S T

Italian Coconut Cream Cake

1 cup (2 sticks) softened butter	1 cup nuts
2 cups sugar	5 egg whites, stiffly beaten
5 egg yolks	5 tablespoons flour
2 cups all-purpose flour	1 cup milk
1 teaspoon baking soda	1 cup sugar
1 cup buttermilk	1 cup softened butter
1 teaspoon vanilla	1 teaspoon vanilla
one 3½-ounce can coconut	¼ cup coconut

Preheat oven to 250°. Butter and flour cake pan(s).

Cream butter and sugar. Beat in egg yolks one at a time. Blend in flour combined with baking soda, alternating with buttermilk. Add vanilla. Beat just until smooth. Stir in coconut and nuts. Gently fold in egg whites. Bake for 20 minutes.

To make the frosting, cook 5 tablespoons flour and 1 cup milk on low heat until thick, stirring constantly. Cool. Cream butter, sugar and vanilla. Beat flour mixture into creamed butter mixture until it is creamy and of a spreading consistency.

Frost cake and sprinkle top and sides of cake with coconut. Serves 12 to 14.

ANNIE'S BED & BREAKFAST
P.O. Box 928
Big Sandy, Texas
75755
(214) 636-4355

MC/V
Expensive to very expensive

Annie's Bed & Breakfast is a unique east Texas Victorian inn with 13 individually-decorated rooms and is home to Annie's Attic, a national mail-order needlecraft company.

The Wedgwood Inn
New Hope, Pennsylvania

Part 3

TEATIME

The Homestead Inn
Greenwich, Connecticut

Teatime

The venerable British tradition of afternoon tea has begun making its appearance on the American scene. Once the preserve of the upper class, it is now enjoying a popularity as an occasion for intimate discussions, informal get-togethers and even business meetings. Although traditionally held between 3:00 and 5:00 P.M., teatime may begin a bit earlier and even run a bit later. Besides tea, such treats as sandwiches, cakes and pastries, crumpets, scones, shortbreads, petit fours and fruits will tempt those who wish to indulge.

For those inns which have adopted the custom, teatime provides a wonderful opportunity for guests and innkeepers to discuss the day's sightseeing and evening dinner plans. At the Mainstay Inn in Cape May, New Jersey, tea is the time when the guests get to know the innkeeper and one another. Guests gather in the dining room or on the veranda or may choose to take their tea and tidbits outside to sit by the garden fountain. Innkeepers say that many a friendship has been cemented over the rim of a teacup.

Each inn has its own special style of serving tea. Ron Gibson, innkeeper of the Victorian Villa in Union City, Michigan, has researched the custom in antique cookbooks and has become an expert in this afternoon affair. To start with, he offers a choice of 30 different teas, including some which he himself blends. To complement the tea, a vast array of delectables are served: perhaps cheese and crackers, meat or cucumber sandwiches, crumpets, smoked fish, scones, tea breads, pastries and fruit. Ron recommends a change of teas midway through the afternoon: maybe starting with a brisk orange pekoe or English breakfast and then switching to an Earl Grey for the sweets.

L I B E R T Y I N N — 1 8 3 4

Liberty Inn–1834
English Tea Biscuits

1 cup softened butter
2 cups sugar
3 eggs
¾ cup sour cream
1 cup chopped pecans
   (medium-sized pieces)

1 teaspoon vanilla
1 teaspoon baking soda
¼ teaspoon salt
4 cups cake flour

Preheat oven to 425°. Butter a baking dish.

Cream butter and sugar. Add eggs, sour cream, pecans and vanilla, stirring well after each addition. Sift together soda, salt and cake flour. Stir flour mixture into creamed butter and sugar mixture. Place dough on waxed paper and roll into a 1½" rope. Chill or semi-freeze. Cut rope into ¼" slices. Bake 15 to 20 minutes. Cool. Can be stored up to 3 months in airtight cannisters. Makes 4 dozen biscuits.

LIBERTY INN — 1834
128 West Liberty Street
Savannah, Georgia
31401
(912) 233-1007

MC/V/AE
Expensive

A favorite haunt of honey-mooners, the inn's suites bring the romance of old Savannah into the 20th century.

Britt House
San Diego, California

DEVON COTTAGE

Persimmon Bread

½ cup softened butter
¾ cup sugar
2 eggs
1 cup all-purpose flour
1 cup whole wheat flour
1 teaspoon baking soda
1 teaspoon baking powder
½ teaspoon salt

½ teaspoon ginger
1½ teaspoons cinnamon
1 teaspoon nutmeg
1 cup persimmon pulp
2 teaspoons vanilla
½ cup chopped black
  walnuts

Preheat oven to 375°. Butter a 8" by 4" loaf pan.

Cream butter and sugar. Beat in eggs one at a time and set aside. Sift together flours, baking soda, baking powder, salt, ginger, cinnamon and nutmeg. Gradually blend dry mixture into butter mixture. Add persimmon pulp, vanilla and walnuts, and mix just until a stiff dough forms. Spoon dough into loaf pan. Bake for 50 minutes to one hour or until tests done. Serve sliced, with cream cheese. Yields one loaf, which serves 10 to 15.

DEVON COTTAGE
26 Eureka Street
Eureka Springs, Arkansas
72632
(501) 253-9169

No credit cards
Moderate

Located on a hilltop in the heart of the Ozark Mountains, the Devon Cottage is a homey, 2 guest-room inn offering hammocks and hospitality. The entire town of Eureka Springs is listed on the National Register of Historic Places.

THE PRESTON HOUSE

Scottish Currant Shortbread

⅓ cups currants or raisins
5 tablespoons fresh orange
  juice
1½ cups all-purpose flour

2 tablespoons sugar
½ cup (1 stick) chilled
  unsalted butter

Preheat oven to 350°. Lightly butter baking sheet.

Bring currants or raisins and 4 tablespoons orange juice to boil in small saucepan, stirring. Remove from heat and let cool. Combine flour and sugar in large bowl. Cut in butter till mixture resembles coarse meal. Stir in fruit mixture and remaining tablespoon orange juice. Knead just till dough holds together. Roll dough out on prepared baking sheet into 10" by 12" rectangle. Trim edges and square off corners. Prick surface all over with fork. Sprinkle with sugar. Cut into 24 squares, leaving in place on baking sheet. Bake till pale golden color, 20 to 22 minutes. Re-cut while warm. Cool on rack, then store in airtight container. Yields 24 pieces.

THE PRESTON HOUSE
106 Faithway Street
Santa Fe, New Mexico
87501
(505) 982-3465

MC/V
Expensive

Listed on the National Register of Historic Places, the Preston House, just off the Old Santa Fe Trail, is a Queen Anne-style house filled with antiques, fireplaces, fresh flowers and fruit.

Whitegate Inn
Mendocino, California

W I L D W O O D   I N N

Wildwood's Tea Scones

2 cups sifted all-purpose flour	½ teaspoon salt
2 tablespoons sugar	⅓ cup butter
3 teaspoons baking powder	½ to ¾ cup milk
	1 egg, lightly beaten (optional)

Preheat oven to 425°. Butter a cookie sheet.

Sift flour, sugar, baking powder and salt together. Work in butter until particles are the size of coarse cornmeal. Combine egg and about ½ cup milk. Stir liquids quickly and lightly into the dry ingredients until dough is moistened. The less milk the better, but add a little more if needed, to make a soft dough.

Grease your hands and turn the dough out onto a floured dish towel. Knead gently 15 times. Cut dough in half. Shape each half into a ball and press down to form a round, approximately ¼" thick. Cut each into 8 wedges, like a pie, using a floured knife. Place wedges on a greased cookie sheet or pie tin, without allowing them to touch. Bake for 10 to 15 minutes. If you'd like them to shine, glaze with lightly-beaten egg before baking. Scones should be golden brown when done. Yields 16 scones, which serve 6 to 8.

THE WILDWOOD INN
121 Church Street
Ware, Massachusetts
01082
(413) 967-7798

MC/V/AE
Moderate

The Wildwood Inn is a place to relax and unwind—and maybe take a bicycle ride, a plunge in the swimming hole, a hike or a walk down the local shady lanes. Its unusual collection of American primitive antiques and heirloom quilts make it the perfect backdrop for a visit to nearby Old Sturbridge Village.

THE VICTORIAN VILLA

Hazelnut and Currant Scones

2 cups all-purpose flour
2 teaspoons baking
  powder
½ cup sugar
⅓ cup butter

2 eggs
¼ cup milk
½ cup chopped hazelnuts
½ cup Zante currants
  (dried)

Preheat oven to 375°. Line baking sheet with parchment paper.

Mix flour, baking powder and sugar. Rub butter into the flour mixture. Beat together eggs and milk, and stir into dry ingredients. Add hazelnuts and currants. Knead mixture 20 times, and roll out ½" to ¾" thick. Cut scones with a fluted round biscuit cutter. Bake for 12 to 18 minutes. Serves 8.

THE VICTORIAN VILLA
601 North Broadway
Union City, Michigan
49094
(517) 741-7383

MC/V
Moderate to expensive

The Victorian Villa is a 19th-century mansion run by innkeepers who are established experts on the custom of afternoon tea.

THE MAINSTAY INN

Eccles Cakes

1¾ cup all-purpose flour
2½ teaspoons baking
  powder
1 tablespoon sugar
¼ teaspoon salt
¼ cup (½ stick) chilled
  butter

2 eggs
⅓ cup light cream
currants or chopped dates
butter and sugar

Preheat oven to 450°. Butter a baking sheet.

Mix flour, baking powder, sugar and salt together. Work butter into flour mixture to form pea-sized pieces. Beat eggs, and reserve two tablespoons of beaten egg. Stir cream into larger quantity of the eggs. Make a large well in the center of flour mixture. Add egg/cream and stir until just blended. Turn out onto a floured board, and knead until the dough loses its stickiness. Roll out to ¾" thickness, and cut into 2½" rounds. Place 1½" apart on the baking sheet. Poke a hole in the center of each round, and fill with currants or chopped dates. Dot each with butter. Fold opposite edges of circle together, and pinch edges closed like a turnover, sealing in filling. Brush tops with reserved egg and sprinkle with sugar. Bake for 12 minutes. Yields one dozen cakes.

THE MAINSTAY INN
635 Columbia Avenue
Cape May, New Jersey
08204
(609) 884-8690

No credit cards
Expensive

The Mainstay Inn was built by two wealthy 19th-century gamblers who spared no expense in its construction.

HISTORIC 1725 WITMER'S TAVERN

Lafayette's Rice Cake

General Lafayette acquired his taste for this cake while recuperating in Bethlehem, Pennsylvania, at the Sun Inn during the Valley Forge winter encampment. Wherever he travelled and found Mennonite cooks, he requested it. At Historic 1725 Witmer's Tavern, this dessert is now served on special occasions.

1 cup softened butter	¼ teaspoon nutmeg
2 cups sugar	2 tablespoons rum or
4 egg yolks	brandy
2 cups rice flour	1 cup milk
1 cup wheat flour	4 egg whites, stiffly beaten
1 teaspoon baking powder	powdered sugar (optional)

Preheat oven to 350°. Butter Turk's-head mold (or loaf tin) and lightly dust with flour.

Cream butter and sugar. Add yolks one at a time, beating until creamy. In another bowl, sift rice and wheat flours together with baking powder and nutmeg. Combine rum or brandy with milk in a cup. Blend flour mixture into creamed butter mixture. Gently beat in milk and liquor combination, stopping when a smooth consistency is reached. Fold in beaten egg whites. Transfer to mold and bake for one hour. Cool 15 minutes before removing from pan. Sprinkle powdered sugar over cooled cake, if desired. Yields one cake, which serves 8 to 10.

HISTORIC 1725
WITMER'S TAVERN
2014 Old Philadelphia Pike
Lancaster, Pennsylvania
17602
(717) 299-5305

No credit cards
Moderate to expensive

In the heart of the Pennsylvania Dutch country, the tavern was the starting point for many westward wagon trains and is listed on the National Register of Historic Places.

*Longswamp B & B
Mertztown, Pennsylvania*

Poppy Seed Tea Cake

½ pound softened butter
1 cup sugar
4 egg yolks
¼ cup poppy seeds
2 cups cake flour

1 teaspoon baking soda
½ pint (1 cup) sour cream
4 egg whites, stiffly beaten
1 teaspoon almond extract
1 teaspoon cinnamon

Preheat oven to 350°. Butter a tube pan and lightly dust with flour.

Cream together butter, sugar, egg yolks and poppy seeds. Sift together flour and baking soda. Add flour mixture and sour cream alternately to creamed mixture, beginning and ending with flour mixture. Combine egg whites, almond extract and cinnamon and fold into batter.

Pour into tube pan. Bake for one hour or until cake tester comes out clean. Cool on cake rack. Serves 8 to 10.

RED CLOVER INN
Woodward Road
Mendon, Vermont
05701
(802) 775-2290

MC/V/AE/DC
Moderate to expensive

The Red Clover Inn is a country estate hidden in a valley down a country road. The owner, who is also the chef, delights guests with candlelit breakfasts.

*The Foxes Bed & Breakfast Inn
Sutter Creek, California*

LONGSWAMP BED & BREAKFAST

Carrot-Zucchini Bread

2½ cups unsifted all-purpose flour	1½ cups buttermilk
1 cup unsifted whole wheat flour	2 tablespoons melted butter
1 tablespoon baking powder	grated rinds of 1 orange and 1 lemon
1 teaspoon baking soda	1 cup coarsely shredded zucchini
½ teaspoon salt	1 cup coarsely shredded carrots
½ cup firmly packed brown sugar	whipped cream cheese
2 eggs	powdered ginger

Preheat oven to 350°. Butter a 9″ by 5″ by 3″ loaf pan.

Mix together flours, baking powder, soda, salt and sugar. Add remaining ingredients. Stir until well blended. Pour into loaf pan and bake for 1¼ hours or until cake is firm. Cool 5 minutes, then unmold onto a rack. Cool before slicing. When cool, top with whipped cream cheese flavored with a touch of powdered ginger. Yields one loaf, which serves 10.

LONGSWAMP B & B
R.D. 2, Box 26
Mertztown, Pennsylvania
19539
(215) 682-6197

No credit cards
Moderate

This rural inn was once a stop on the underground railway for slaves escaping the South.

TAUGHANNOCK FARMS INN

Orange Date Bread

rind of 1 orange	1 cup (2 sticks) butter
1 cup water	2 cups all-purpose flour
½ cup chopped dates	2 teaspoons baking powder
¾ cup sugar	½ teaspoon salt
2 tablespoons butter	
1 egg, beaten	

Preheat oven to 350°. Generously butter an 8″ by 4″ loaf pan.

Mix together the first 3 ingredients in a saucepan and boil gently. Add sugar and butter, stir until dissolved and remove from heat. When cooled, stir in remaining ingredients. Put in loaf pan and bake for about 45 minutes or until it tests done. Serve sliced, with cream cheese. Yields one loaf, which serves 8 to 10.

TAUGHANNOCK
FARMS INN
R.D. 3
Trumansburg, New York
14886

No credit cards
Moderate

The Taughannock Farms Inn is set among some of central New York State's most spectacular scenery: Taughannock Falls and Gorge and Cayuga Lake.

Grant Corner Inn
Santa Fe, New Mexico

THE RAY HOUSE

Ray House Lemon Loaf

1 stick (4 ounces) softened
* butter*
1 cup sugar
2 eggs
1½ cups bread or
* all-purpose flour*
1 teaspoon baking powder
¼ teaspoon salt
1 tablespoon grated lemon
* rind*
½ cup milk
lemon sauce (see following
* recipe)*

Preheat oven to 350°. Butter and flour a 8½" by 4½" loaf pan.

Cream butter and sugar by hand in a large bowl. Add eggs, one at a time, beating after each addition. Sift flour, baking powder and salt onto sheet of waxed paper. With fork, stir in lemon rind. Add flour mixture and milk to batter alternately, beginning and ending with the flour mixture.

Pour into loaf pan. Bake for one hour or until cake tester comes out clean. Pour lemon sauce over hot cake. Allow it to cool for 10 minutes, then turn out on rack to cool completely. Yields one loaf. Keeps for one week when well-wrapped and refrigerated.

LEMON SAUCE:
⅓ cup sugar
¼ cup fresh lemon juice

Stir sugar into lemon juice until it dissolves.

THE RAY HOUSE
83 Hillside Street
Asheville, North Carolina
28801
(704) 252-0106

No credit cards
Moderate

Located in the Blue Ridge Mountain town of Asheville, the 3-room Ray House has the atmosphere of an English country home and a library stocked with lots of good books.

Chocolate Ribbon Cake

½ cup (1 stick) softened
  butter
1 cup sugar
2 cups all-purpose flour
1 teaspoon baking powder
  (double-acting)
1 teaspoon baking soda
1 teaspoon vanilla

one 8-ounce container
  sour cream
2 eggs
½ teaspoon ground
  cinnamon
2 squares semisweet
  chocolate, grated

Preheat oven to 350°. Butter and lightly flour a 9" by 5" loaf pan or 10" bundt pan (a fluted tube cake pan).

In large bowl with mixer at medium speed, beat butter and sugar until light and fluffy. Reduce speed to low. Add flour, baking powder, baking soda, vanilla extract, sour cream and eggs. Beat just until blended, scraping down bowl as necessary. Increase speed to medium, beat one minute, occasionally scraping down bowl. Spread half of the batter evenly in pan. Sprinkle with half of the grated chocolate and ¼ teaspoon cinnamon. Repeat with remaining batter, grated chocolate and cinnamon. Draw knife through batter a few times to swirl chocolate. Bake one hour, or until cake tester inserted in center comes out clean. Cool in pan on wire rack 10 minutes. Serve warm, or let cake cool completely on wire rack. Makes one loaf, which serves 16.

COUNTRY INN
632 North Main Street
Fort Bragg, California
95437
(707) 964-3737

MC/V/AE
Moderate

Built in the 1800s, the Country Inn is centrally located in the northern California coastal town of Fort Bragg, within walking distance of restaurants, galleries, shops and the beach.

Victorian Date Nut Bread

1 pound dates, coarsely
  chopped
1 pound pecans, coarsely
  chopped
1 cup sugar

1 cup all-purpose flour
1 teaspoon vanilla
2 teaspoons baking
  powder
4 eggs

Preheat oven to 350°. Butter an 8" by 4" by 2" loaf pan and lightly dust with flour.

Mix together dates and nuts. Add sugar, flour, vanilla and baking powder, and mix until blended. Add eggs and continue stirring until batter is evenly moistened. Place batter in pan and bake for one hour. Yields one loaf, serving 8 to 10.

COUNTRY INN AT
PRINCETON
30 Mountain Road
Princeton, Massachusetts
01541
(617) 464-2030

MC/V/AE
Very expensive

Located on 12 acres of lovely lawn and gardens, the Country Inn has 6 large parlor suites and 3 dining rooms serving haute cuisine.

THE NATIONAL HOUSE INN

Sesame Seed Bread or Bars

½ cup sesame seeds
½ cup (1 stick) softened
  butter
1¼ cups all-purpose flour
1 teaspoon baking powder

½ teaspoon salt
1 cup brown sugar
2 eggs
1 teaspoon vanilla

Preheat oven to 375°. Butter 2 small loaf pans.

Toast sesame seeds. Remove from heat. Cream butter and stir in sesame seeds. Sift together flour, baking powder, and salt. Beat sugar, eggs and vanilla into butter mixture. Stir in mixture of dry ingredients. Bake in the 2 loaf pans for 25 minutes or until center of loaves test done with a toothpick.

You may also make sesame seed bars by spreading mixture in a greased square pan and baking. Cut into bars while warm. Serves 9 to 12.

THE NATIONAL HOUSE INN
102 South Parkview
Marshall, Michigan
49068
(616) 781-7374

MC/V/AE
Expensive

In the historic southern Michigan town of Marshall, the National House Inn has the distinction of being the state's oldest inn.

HEADLANDS INN

Headlands Inn Lemon Bread

1 cup softened butter
2 cups sugar
4 eggs
½ teaspoon salt
½ teaspoon soda
3 cups all-purpose flour

1 cup buttermilk
1 cup chopped nuts
grated rind of 1 lemon
juice of 3 lemons
1 cup sugar

Preheat oven to 350°. Butter and flour two 7" by 3" by 2" loaf pans.

Cream butter and 2 cups sugar. Beat in eggs, one at a time. Sift together salt, soda, and flour, and add alternately, with the buttermilk, to the creamed butter and sugar. Begin and end with the dry ingredients. Fold in the nuts and rind. Bake for 40 minutes to one hour or until tests done.

Heat lemon juice and sugar long enough for the sugar to dissolve. Place warm loaves of bread on foil and spoon juice topping over them. Yields 2 loaves, each of which serves 8.

HEADLANDS INN
P.O. Box 132
Mendocino, California
95460
(707) 937-4431

No credit cards
Expensive

A comfortable restored Victorian home nestled in a northern California village, the Headlands has many rooms with ocean views.

THE BRITT HOUSE

White Bread

Great for tea sandwiches.

¼ *cup butter, melted and cooled slightly*	*2 teaspoons salt (optional)*
1 tablespoon sugar	*2 cups water, lukewarm*
2 tablespoons yeast	*up to 6 cups all-purpose flour*

Combine first five ingredients and mix well. Gradually add up to 6 cups flour, a cup at a time, until the dough forms a ball and leaves the sides of the bowl. Turn onto floured surface and knead until dough becomes elastic to the touch, yet is soft as a baby's cheek. Turn into a greased bowl and let rise in warm spot until doubled in bulk. Shape into 2 standard loaves in loaf pans, or divide into eight 3″ by 5″ pans. Let rise again until double. Bake at 350° for 20 minutes or until golden and hollow at the top. Yields 2 loaves, approximately 20 slices each.

Shortbread

1 pound (4 sticks) softened unsalted butter	*1 cup sugar*
	4½ cups all-purpose flour

Preheat oven to 250°. Butter four 9″ pie pans.

Cream together butter and sugar. Add flour, and with hands force mixture together. (A mixer does not work well for this process.) Divide and pat into 4 pie pans. The dough should be about ½″ thick. Pierce in several places with a fork. Score into 16 triangles. (Shortbread is scored raw, then it breaks easily along these lines when baked.) Bake for 1½ to 2 hours, or until slightly golden. Yields 64 pieces.

THE BRITT HOUSE
406 Maple Street
San Diego, California
92103
(619) 234-2926

MC/V
Expensive

Located just 2 blocks from Balboa Park, the Britt House has individually-named and decorated rooms, as well as a separate cottage. Fruit and home-made cookies greet new arrivals, and a formal afternoon tea is served in the parlor.

Williams House
Hot Springs National Park, Arkansas

PUDDING CREEK INN

Sugar Crisp Twisties

1 package active dry yeast
¼ cup lukewarm water
3½ cups sifted all-purpose
   flour
1½ teaspoon salt
1 cup (2 sticks) chilled
   butter

2 eggs, lightly beaten
½ cup sour cream
3 teaspoons vanilla
1½ cup sugar

Preheat oven to 375°.

Proof yeast in warm water. Sift flour and salt into mixing bowl. Cut in butter until particles are fine. Blend in eggs, sour cream, one teaspoon vanilla and yeast. Mix well. Cover and chill at least 2 hours. (Dough may be stored in refrigerator for up to 4 days, shaped and baked as needed.) Combine sugar and 2 teaspoons vanilla. Sprinkle ½ cup on rolling surface. Roll out half the dough on vanilla-sugar mixture to a 16" by 8" shape. Sprinkle with about one tablespoon of the vanilla-sugar. Fold one end of the dough over the center, then fold other end to make 3 layers. Turn dough ¼ of the way around, repeat rolling, folding and sprinkling. Roll out to 16" by 8". Cut into strips. Twist each strip 2 or 3 times. Place on ungreased cookie sheets. Repeat process with remaining dough and vanilla-sugar mixture. Bake for 15 to 20 minutes until golden brown. Serves 8 to 10.

PUDDING CREEK INN

Cheese Fingers

16 ounces softened cream
  cheese
½ cup sugar
4 egg yolks
1 teaspoon vanilla or
  almond extract

1 box phyllo dough
½ pound (2 sticks) butter,
  melted
chopped almonds
  (optional)

Preheat oven to 375°.

Blend together cream cheese, sugar, egg yolks and vanilla or almond extract to make the filling. Unwrap phyllo dough and cover with damp towel, so that the dough doesn't dry out. Lay out one sheet of dough and brush with melted butter. Fold over the top half of the sheet. Brush again with butter. Put 2 teaspoons of filling at one long end. Take wide ends and fold ½" in on each side. Starting at filling end, roll up into a "finger." Brush with butter. Put seam-side down on ungreased cookie sheet. Sprinkle with almonds, if desired. Repeat with remaining dough and filling. Bake for 10 to 15 minutes, or until brown. Serves 6 to 8.

PUDDING CREEK INN
700 North Main Street
Fort Bragg, California
95437
(707) 964-9529

MC/V
Moderate

At the Pudding Creek Inn, built in 1884 by a Russian count, breakfast is served in an enclosed flower-filled fountain courtyard.

MACLEAN HOUSE

Scottish Shortbread

1 pound (4 sticks) softened
  unsalted butter
1 cup powdered sugar
3 cups sifted all-purpose
  flour

1 cup rice flour (or
  substitute 1 additional
  cup all-purpose flour)

Preheat oven to 275°.

Cream butter and sugar. Blend well, but don't overwork. Gradually add flour. Turn dough on board lightly dusted with a mixture of powdered sugar and flour. Pat dough or roll gently into a 7" by 10" rectangle, ⅜" thick. Place on baking sheet. Prick with fork. Mark with cutting lines. Refrigerate till cold. Cut apart and bake for about 40 minutes, until shortbread is sand-colored. Yields 20 pieces.

MACLEAN HOUSE
P.O. Box 651
Inverness, California
94937
(415) 669-7392
Reservations:
(415) 663-1420

No credit cards
Moderate

This small, quiet, secluded guest house on Tomales Bay just north of San Francisco greets its guests with sherry and shortbread.

Petticoat Tails

1½ cups (3 sticks) butter
1 cup granulated sugar
2 teaspoons vanilla
1½ tablespoon milk

3¾ cups unsifted
  all-purpose flour
3 tablespoons powdered
  sugar (optional)

Preheat oven to 325°.

With electric mixer, beat butter, sugar and vanilla until light and fluffy. Stir in milk and flour using a wooden spoon, then mix with hand until dough is smooth. Divide dough into 3 parts. On ungreased cookie sheets, roll out dough, one part at a time, into ¼" thick 9" rounds. Place 7" plate in centers of rounds, and cut around plate with a fluted pastry cutter. Remove plate. Cut into eight sections. Bake 25 minutes. Cool completely. Sprinkle with confectioner's sugar if desired.

CLEFTSTONE MANOR
92 Eden Street
Bar Harbor, Maine
04609
(207) 288-4951

MC/V/AE
Moderate to expensive

Located on a windswept cliff at the foot of Cadillac Mountain, the century-old Cleftstone Manor offers a relaxing refuge from everyday life.

Lamothe House Pecan Pralines

1½ cups granulated sugar
½ cup brown sugar
½ stick (4 tablespoons)
  butter
½ cup evaporated milk

1 teaspoon vanilla
½ cup chopped or whole
  pecans
1 pinch baking soda

Butter cookie sheet or line with waxed paper.

Cook sugars and milk over medium heat, stirring until mixture starts to boil. Add butter, pecans and soda. Cook, stirring occasionally until it reaches the soft ball stage (when a bit of the candy dropped in cold water forms a soft ball) or 238° on a candy thermometer. Remove from fire and beat with spoon until mixture is creamy and begins to thicken. Drop by teaspoonfuls onto cookie sheet. (If mixture becomes too hard, return to heat and add a little water.) Makes 12 large or 24 small pralines.

LAMOTHE HOUSE
621 Esplanade Avenue
New Orleans, Louisiana
70116
(504) 947-1161

MC/V/AE
Very expensive

One of New Orleans's classic bed and breakfast inns, the Lamothe House captures all the charm of the city's French Quarter.

Strawberry Preserves

4 cups strawberries, cleaned and hulled	3 cups sugar

To make more or less preserves, use ¾ cup sugar for every cup of strawberries. Place strawberries in a bowl, layering with sugar. Allow to stand for 12 hours. In a saucepan, bring quickly to boiling point and simmer for 15 minutes. Place in a crock or enamel bowl, cover and allow to steep for another 12 hours. Return to pot just to reheat, then put the preserves in sterilized jars. Seal with paraffin. Yields 2 pints.

Orange Marmalade

2 large oranges	11 cups water
2 large lemons	8 cups sugar

Cut fruit into quarters and remove seeds. Soak the fruit in the water for 24 hours. Drain, reserving the liquid. Cut pulp into shreds. Return to the soaking water and boil for one hour. Add the sugar. Boil until juice forms a jelly. Cool, and put in hot sterilized jars. Seal with paraffin. (Add more lemons if a tarter marmalade is preferred. Emily Hunter at Briar Rose makes her marmalade on the tart side and uses coarsely cut rind.) Yields 2 quarts.

BRIAR ROSE
BED & BREAKFAST
2151 Arapahoe Avenue
Boulder, Colorado
80302
(303) 442-3007

MC/V/AE
Moderate to expensive

Guests at this English country-style home find chocolates on their pillows at bedtime and a decanter of sherry always proffered in the dining room.

Millbrook, A Country Inn
Waitsfield, Vermont

THE OKEMO INN

Bourbon Slush

2 cups boiling water
4 tea bags
2 cups sugar
7 cups cold water
2 cups bourbon

one 6-ounce can frozen
  lemonade concentrate
one 12-ounce can frozen
  orange juice concentrate
12 sprigs of mint

Combine the boiling water with the tea bags and allow to steep 4 to 5 minutes. Add the sugar, cold water, bourbon and 2 frozen juice concentrates in a large bowl or pot. Mix all together well, until frozen juice concentrates are fully thawed and blended. Pour into a large plastic bowl or other unbreakable container, and place in the freezer overnight.

To serve, spoon "slush" into four 6-ounce serving cups or glasses, and garnish each with a sprig of mint. Serve with a spoon. Serves 12. Keeps indefinitely in the freezer.

THE OKEMO INN
R.F.D. 1, Box 133
Ludlow, Vermont
05149
(802) 228-8834

All major credit cards
Moderate

Named after the mountain that towers in the background, the 12-room Okemo Inn offers summer golf and winter ski packages.

BISHOPSGATE INN

Minted Raspberry Cooler

½ cup fresh mint leaves
  plus mint sprigs for
  garnish
1 cup boiling water
one 6-ounce can frozen
  lemonade concentrate

1 pint fresh raspberries
  crushed and sweetened
  with ½ cup sugar (or
  one 10-ounce package
  frozen raspberries)
2 cups cold water

Combine ½ cup mint leaves and boiling water. Let steep 5 minutes. Add raspberries and frozen lemonade concentrate. Stir (until thawed, if frozen raspberries are used). Strain into pitcher half-filled with crushed ice. Add cold water and stir. Garnish with fresh mint leaves. Serves 8.

BISHOPSGATE INN
Goodspeed Landing
East Haddam, Connecticut
06423
(203) 873-1677

No credit cards
Moderate

Within walking distance of the famous Goodspeed Opera House, this 1818 colonial home is also near many sites of historical interest.

Champagne Punch

2 cups sugar
4 cups water
½ cup lemon juice
½ cup lime juice

4½ cups orange juice
2 cups grapefruit juice
2 cups Rhine wine
1 bottle champagne

In a saucepan, combine sugar with 2 cups water and lemon juice and boil one minute. Add remaining water and let cool. Stir in lime, orange and grapefruit juices. Pour into bowl filled with ice. Add wine and champagne just before serving. Yields approximately 30 servings.

INNSBRUCK INN
233 West Main Street
Aspen, Colorado
81611
(303) 925-2980

MC/V/AE/CB/DC
Expensive to very
expensive

At the family-operated Innsbruck Inn, guests will enjoy a breakfast buffet before a busy day on the slopes, and a sauna and glass of wine après ski. Many friendships are formed here, and groups return together year after year.

Anna's Lemonade

2½ cups honey (star
    thistle or other light
    honey)
2½ cups water
2 cups fresh lemon juice,
    or to taste

water
3 tablespoons spearmint
    leaves

Blend honey, 2½ cups water and lemon juice in a blender. Put in a gallon container. Fill to three quarters of a gallon with additional water. Add spearmint leaves and allow to steep. Serve over ice. Yields 16 cups.

HARBIN HOT SPRINGS
P.O. Box 782
Middletown, California
95461
(707) 987-2477

No credit cards
Inexpensive to moderate

This 1,100-acre bathing-suit-optional hot springs resort is set in the hills just above northern California's Napa Valley.

*Center Lovell Inn
Center Lovell, Maine*

SHELBURNE INN

Lemon Curd

Originally created as a tea-time condiment for scones and crumpets, lemon curd is also delicious on muffins, toast, waffles or pancakes.

*1 cup fresh-squeezed
lemon juice*
*7 tablespoons lemon zest
(the outermost part of
lemon rind)*

*1 pound (about 2 cups)
sugar*
¼ pound (1 stick) butter
8 eggs, lightly beaten

Combine lemon juice, zest, sugar and butter in double boiler over simmering water until sugar dissolves and butter melts. Whisk eggs into lemon mixture and keep stirring until thick (about 20 minutes). Remove from heat, cool and store in refrigerator. Yields about 5 cups.

THE SHELBURNE INN
Pacific Highway 103 and
J Street
Seaview, Washington
98644
(206) 642-2442

MC/V
Expensive

Located on the Pacific coast in the southwest corner of Washington state, the Shelburne Inn has 14 rooms and a restaurant that serves nationally-acclaimed cuisine.

*Mayhurst
North Garden, Virginia*

GUSTAVUS INN

Raspberry Shrub

cider vinegar   sugar
raspberries   soda water or cold water

Pour enough cider vinegar over raspberries to cover the berries. Let this stand, covered with a clean cloth, for 24 hours to two days. Strain through a couple thicknesses of cheesecloth, squeezing the berries to extract all the juice. To every pint of liquid, add a scant cup of sugar. Bring to a boil, and boil gently for 20 minutes. Let cool slightly, and pour into glass jars or bottles. Keep in a cool, dark place until needed. Serve as a beverage, pouring two tablespoons of the shrub over ice cubes and filling the glass to the top with cold water or soda water. Each cup of shrub makes 8 drinks.

Spruce Tip Beer

green tips of spruce   boiling water
   branches (gathered in   sugar
   early spring)*   yeast

In early spring, gather a peck of new bright green tips of the spruce branches. Cover with boiling water, and let the mixture cool. Drain the liquid from the spruce tips and to 2½ gallons of the liquid add 2 pounds of sugar and ⅛ teaspoon of yeast dissolved in 2 tablespoons of water. Stir all together until sugar and yeast are completely dissolved. Bottle immediately and store in a warm place for four or five days before opening. Chill bottles before opening. Each gallon fills about ten 12-ounce bottles. This is a cooling non-alcoholic drink.

*If spruce tips are gathered when no longer tiny and new, the beer will take on a strong flavor and will be so effervescent that the bottles may burst.

GUSTAVUS INN
Box 31-B
Gustavus, Alaska
99826
(907) 697-3311

No credit cards
Expensive

This 7-room summertime Glacier Bay inn offers delightful local dishes, with fresh fish and eggs, vegetables picked from the garden, and berries for jam plucked from bushes in nearby fields and forests.

Lone Mountain Ranch
Big Sky, Montana

CAPTAIN JEFFERDS INN

Holiday Hot Mulled Wine

3 whole allspice
6 whole cloves
5 cinnamon sticks
2 cups water
½ cup sugar

2 lemons, seeded and
thinly sliced
1 bottle claret (or
comparable red wine)

Enclose allspice, cloves and cinnamon sticks in cheesecloth and tie. Combine 2 cups water with sugar, add bag of spices and bring mixture to a boil. Lower heat and simmer for 10 minutes. Remove from burner. Add lemon slices, cover, and let the mixture stand for at least 20 minutes. Add claret and cook over medium heat until hot but not boiling for 10 minutes. Remove spice bag and serve. Serves 6.

CAPTAIN JEFFERDS INN
P.O. Box 691
Kennebunkport, Maine
04046
(207) 967-2311

No credit cards
Moderate to expensive

This mansion, a former sea captain's residence, was built in 1804. Captain Jefferds' 11 rooms are filled with antiques, art, and flowers, and the inn allows pets, if well-behaved.

Hot Buttered Wedgwood

Carl Glassman makes his own liqueur, which he calls Wedgwood Almond Liqueur, to use in this recipe. A carafe of the liqueur is served to guests at their bedside as part of the evening ritual.

2 ounces almond liqueur
1 cup hot tea, cider or
   apple juice
1 tablespoon whipped
   unsalted butter

twist of orange peel
cinnamon stick

Pour almond liqueur in a mug. Fill with hot tea, cider or juice. Add butter and orange peel twist. Garnish with a cinnamon stick.

THE WEDGWOOD INN
111 West Bridge Street
New Hope, Pennsylvania
18938
(215) 862-2570

No credit cards
Moderate to expensive

The innkeepers of this Victorian mansion in New Hope promise to make their guests' stays as pleasant as the surroundings.

Victorian Villa Wassail

The Victorian Villa has a very special Christmas season which is celebrated Dickens-style, with wassail, plum puddings, trifles, hickory nut cakes and roasted chestnuts.

1 gallon fresh apple juice
1 quart fresh strained
   cranberry juice
1½ cups sugar
1 tablespoon aromatic
   bitters

4 cinnamon sticks
1 tablespoon whole
   allspice
2 oranges studded with
   cloves
2 cups dark rum

Combine ingredients and heat gently. Serve warm. Serves 20 to 25.

THE VICTORIAN VILLA
601 North Broadway
Union City, Michigan
49094
(517) 741-7383

MC/V
Moderate to expensive

The Victorian Villa is a 19th-century mansion run by innkeepers who are established experts on the custom of afternoon tea.

C I D E R   M I L L

Hot Spiced Cider

On frosty weekends in the fall and winter, Cider Mill keeps their hot spiced cider hot in an electric percolator, so it will be ready for all visitors. On extra cold nights servings are fortified with a shot of rum.

2 teaspoons whole cloves
2 teaspoons whole allspice
2 sticks cinnamon
  (3" each)

1 gallon apple cider
⅔ cup sugar
2 whole oranges, washed

Tie spices in cheesecloth or place in a tea ball. Pour cider in a large pot (a stock pot works well) and add spices, sugar, and oranges. Heat to boiling. Cover and simmer for 20 minutes.

CIDER MILL
P.O. Box 441
Zoar, Ohio
44697
(216) 874-3133

MC/V
Moderate

A renovated mill built in 1863 houses this 2-room inn, located in the heart of northern Ohio's Amish country.

D E E P   C R E E K   L O D G E

Crab Apple Liqueur

1 pound red crab apples
  (approximately)
  per quart jar

1 cup sugar per quart jar
2 cups vodka (approx-
  imately) per quart jar

Wash and remove stems from ripe red crab apples. Cut into quarters. Pack into quart jars up to an inch from the top. Add one cup sugar to each jar. Pour vodka over apples and sugar until it just reaches the surface. Seal the jars. Place sealed jars on their sides in a cool storage room. Turn once a day for 25 to 28 days. Then strain the liquid through a sieve and again through a fine strainer. When you are satisfied with its clarity, bottle in clean gin or vodka bottles. For a clearer drink, you may want to decant it after a few days. Do not throw away the pulp, but put it back into the jars, and carefully pour off the remaining liquid. Eventually when there is very little setting out, you can discard the pulp.

DEEP CREEK INN
Bonners Ferry, Idaho
83805
(208) 267-2373

MC/V
Inexpensive

This family-oriented 12-room country inn overlooks a creek in a setting that is appealing in any season. Guests can enjoy the landscape on the inn's bicycles.

Part 4

HORS D'OEUVRES

Linden Inn
Natchez, Mississippi

Hors d'Oeuvres

Many of the recipes in the preceding chapter on tea are also suitable for hors d'oeuvres. Indeed many inns offer sherry or other wines right along with tea, forming a consolidated teatime–cocktail hour. Inns that follow the custom of wine and hors d'oeuvres usually do so between 6:00 and 8:00 P.M., when guests have had a chance to relax in their rooms and change into evening clothes, then congregate for a little conviviality before a night on the town.

Innkeepers at the Wedgwood in New Hope, Pennsylvania, serve a house liqueur in their blue-and-cream-colored parlor. While sipping a Wedgwood liqueur, one can sit in the bay window and chat with a friend or play Scrabble® or Trivial Pursuit.®

San Francisco's Petite Auberge offers hors d'oeuvres around the fireplace in the lower parlor. Guests gather to discuss their day in the city and make plans for dinner that evening.

The hors d'oeuvres dishes in this book will be interesting additions to your next party tray. With such selections as Smoked Trout Paté, Tom's Treat, *Huîtres des Gourmets*, and Goat Cheese Turnovers, you'll be able to introduce your guests to some exciting new treats.

Arlene's Artichokes

cooking oil for deep frying
30 artichoke hearts,
    parboiled; or 3 cans of
    artichokes packed in
    water (approximately 10
    per can), drained
6 eggs, lightly beaten

2 cups Italian
    bread crumbs
1½ cups (3 sticks) butter
juice of 1½ lemons
3 cloves garlic, minced
3 teaspoons minced chives
Parmesan cheese to taste

Heat oil for frying.

Cut artichokes in half. Dip in beaten egg and coat with bread crumbs. Deep-fry until golden brown. Put on serving plate and keep warm. Melt butter, add lemon juice, garlic and chives.

Pour butter sauce over artichoke hearts and sprinkle with Parmesan cheese. Serves 6.

SOCIETY HILL HOTEL
OF PHILADELPHIA
Third and Chestnut Streets
Philadelphia, Pennsylvania
19106
(215) 925-1394

MC/V/AE
Expensive

Located in Philadelphia's Historic Park, the Society Hill Hotel offers entertainment at its piano bar and fresh flowers and chocolates in each of its 12 rooms.

Wild Mushroom Paté

½ pound (2 sticks)
    unsalted butter
½ yellow onion, chopped
2 cloves garlic, minced
1½ pounds fresh boletus
    mushrooms, gently
    rinsed and chopped

1 tablespoon fresh parsley
1 tablespoon fresh thyme
½ cup dry white wine
⅛ cup dry sherry
salt and pepper to taste

Melt butter, add onion and garlic, and cook gently for a minute. Add boletus, parsley and thyme, and cook over moderate heat until mushrooms give off their juices. Stir in wine and sherry. Cook, stirring occasionally, until liquid is reduced and thickened slightly. Cool briefly, then purée in food processor until smooth. Season to taste with salt and pepper. Pour into individual ramekins and chill until set. Serve with minced red onion and toast. Serves 4 to 6.

GARLAND'S OAK
CREEK LODGE
P.O. Box 152
Sedona, Arizona
86336
(602) 282-3343

MC/V
Expensive

Garland's Oak Creek Lodge consists of rustic log cabins scattered across lawns amidst apple and peach orchards, with Oak Creek running alongside.

Antipasti

ANCHOVY BUTTER:

1 cup (2 sticks) softened
  unsalted butter
3 tablespoons mashed

anchovy fillets (rinsed
  free of salt)

Whip butter with electric mixer and beat in anchovy fillets. Can be used in sauces or, with a pastry tube, to decorate canapes and vegetables. This recipe and the following serve 10 to 15.

MARINATED CARROTS:

1 pound tender young
  carrots
¾ cup dry white wine
¾ cup white wine vinegar
4 cups water
6 tablespoons oil
2 cloves garlic
small bunch parsley,
  minced

1 teaspoon sugar
1 teaspoon salt
pinch Cayenne pepper
1 teaspoon prepared
  Dijon mustard
1 teaspoon chopped fresh
  basil (or ½ teaspoon
  dry basil)

Wash and scrape carrots and cut into strips. Put wine, wine vinegar, water, oil, garlic cloves, parsley, sugar, salt and Cayenne pepper into small pot. Bring to a boil and simmer approximately 10 minutes or until carrots are cooked *al dente*. Allow to cool in pot. Lift out carrots with slotted spoon and place on a serving dish. Boil liquid marinade down until about 2 cups remain. Mix in mustard and pour over carrots. Sprinkle with basil and chill.

*Captain Mey's
Cape May, New Jersey*

CENTER LOVELL INN

ONIONS IN VINEGAR:

24 small, even-sized white onions
6 small hot peppers

1 tablespoon dried tarragon (or one small bunch)
6 cups boiling white wine vinegar

Peel onions and place in a jar with bits of peppers and tarragon. Cover with boiling vinegar and marinate in a cool place for at least one week. Drain. Again, cover with fresh boiling vinegar, seal and store. Chill before use. Refrigerate jar when opened.

SWEET PEPPERS:

8 red sweet peppers
2 tablespoons red wine vinegar
⅛ cup olive oil

½ teaspoon each, salt and pepper
garlic clove, minced

Roast peppers in the oven, or over the flame of a gas jet, until blackened. Peel off skin under running cold water. Seed, and cut into long strips. Marinate for at least one hour in vinegar, olive oil, salt, pepper and garlic.

CENTER LOVELL INN
Route 5
Center Lovell, Maine
04016
(207) 925-1575

MC/V
Very expensive (includes full-course dinner and breakfast for two)

Located in the heart of the White Mountain National Forest area, this inn is for families and features gourmet Italian cuisine.

SCHNEIDER HAUS

Hot Mustard Sauce

½ cup dry mustard
½ cup white vinegar
1 egg

½ cup sugar
cream cheese and crackers

Mix together dry mustard and white vinegar. Let stand overnight or longer. Beat in egg and sugar. Cook in the top of a double boiler over boiling water for 18 minutes over high heat, stirring to prevent coagulation. Serve over cream cheese with crackers. This quantity of sauce will cover 4 to 8 ounces cream cheese and will keep for a couple of months in the refrigerator.

SCHNEIDER HAUS
Route 100, Box 2834
Duxbury, Vermont
05676
(802) 244-7726

MC/V/AE
Moderate

The 10-room Schneider Haus was built entirely by its innkeepers.

Les Huîtres des Gourmets

duxelles (see following recipe)	12 oysters on the half shell
	3 tablespoons garlic butter

Place oysters on an oven-proof dish. Dab duxelles and garlic butter on each, and bake for 5 minutes. Serve garnished with lemon. Serves 4.

DUXELLES:

1 tablespoon butter	1 tablespoon minced shallots
1 tablespoon minced onion	1 tablespoon heavy cream
½ pound mushrooms, minced	salt and pepper to taste

Melt butter in sauté pan. Sauté onions until they begin to color. Add mushrooms and shallots and cook until liquids are rendered and then evaporate. Add a little cream and cook until reduced to a paste-like consistency. Season with salt and pepper to taste.

Casserole d'Escargots

24 snails	4 tablespoons garlic butter
5 ounces chanterelle mushrooms	½ cup heavy cream
1 tablespoon butter	½ teaspoon (a splash) Pernod (optional)
2 teaspoons minced shallots	

In a sauté pan, sauté snails and chanterelles in butter with shallots. Add garlic butter (see following recipe), let melt, and swirl around pan. Stir in heavy cream and Pernod and allow mixture to reduce somewhat. Sprinkle with chopped parsley and serve at once. Serves 4.

GARLIC BUTTER:

Mince large clove of garlic. Melt ¼ cup of softened butter in small pan. Add garlic, minced parsley, salt and pepper to taste. Refrigerate until ready to use.

HOMESTEAD INN
420 Field Point Road
Greenwich, Connecticut
06830
(203) 869-7500

All major credit cards
Very expensive

Built in 1799, the Homestead Inn is famous for its French cuisine and offers a weekend getaway from New York City, 45 minutes away.

VICTORIAN FARMHOUSE

Toasted Clam Rolls

*three 6½-ounce cans
  minced clams*
*⅓ cup thinly-sliced green
  onion*
½ cup mayonnaise
*6 tablespoons grated
  Parmesan cheese*
*1 teaspoon Worcestershire
  Sauce*

¾ teaspoon garlic powder
*½ teaspoon liquid hot
  pepper seasoning*
*1 large 24-ounce loaf
  thin-sliced sandwich
  bread*
*6 tablespoons melted
  butter*

Preheat oven to 425°. Butter a baking sheet.

Drain clams well, reserving liquid for other cooking uses. Combine clams, green onions, mayonnaise, Parmesan cheese, Worcestershire Sauce, garlic powder and hot pepper seasoning.

Trim crusts from bread slices. With a rolling pin, flatten each slice until very thin. Spread about one tablespoon of clam mixture on each piece of bread, then roll up jellyroll fashion. Brush well with melted butter. Leave whole (for sandwiches) or cut in half (for appetizers). Arrange rolls one inch apart on baking sheet. Bake for 12 minutes, or until lightly browned. Makes 2 dozen finger sandwiches or 4 dozen appetizers.

VICTORIAN
FARMHOUSE
P.O. Box 357
Little River, California
95456

No credit cards
Expensive

This countryside inn is set among orchards and flower gardens.

*Die Heimat Country Inn
Homestead, Iowa*

TROUTBECK

Goat Cheese and Seafood Turnovers

DOUGH:

¼ cup heavy cream   2 cups all-purpose flour
¼ cup sour cream   salt and pepper to taste
1 egg

Combine heavy cream, sour cream and egg, then mix in flour, salt and pepper. Knead dough on floured surface until smooth. Let rest one hour in refrigerator, then roll out ⅛″ thick. Cut circles with a 2″ cookie cutter. While dough is chilling, prepare:

CHEESE FILLING:

½ pound chèvre   pinch of salt
¼ pound muenster   pinch of nutmeg
⅛ teaspoon pepper

Crumble cheese together. Mix in spices and set aside.

SEAFOOD STUFFING:

1 large onion, minced   ⅓ pound clams, chopped
1 small green pepper,   salt and pepper to taste
  diced   pinch each of oregano,
⅓ pound scallops,   cumin and flour
  chopped   2 tablespoons water
⅓ pound shrimp, peeled,
  deveined and chopped

Sauté onion until transparent. Add pepper, seafood, seasonings and water. Cook for 2 minutes while stirring. Set aside and let cool.

ASSEMBLY:

Brush edges of dough circles with water. Place ½ teaspoon of filling in middle. Fold dough over filling, like a turnover. Using the tines of a fork, press along edge of turnover, sealing well. Heat oil for frying. Place turnovers in oil and fry on each side until golden brown. Yields approximately 6 dozen turnovers.

TROUTBECK
Leedsville Road
Amenia, New York
12501
(914) 373-8580

AE
Very expensive

This posh 422-acre country estate operates as an inn on the weekends and a conference center during the week and has been praised by *New York* Magazine, *The New York Times, Good Housekeeping* and *Country Living*.

THE BRAMBLE INN

Caponata

2 pounds eggplant, peeled
   and cubed (½" cubes)
salt
½ cup olive oil
2 cups finely-chopped
   celery
¾ cup finely-chopped
   onions
⅓ cup wine vinegar mixed
   with 4 teaspoons sugar

3 cups drained
   whole-pack tomatoes
2 tablespoons
   tomato paste
6 large green olives,
   pitted and slivered
2 tablespoons capers
4 anchovy fillets, rinsed,
   pounded flat and
   smooth
freshly ground pepper

Sprinkle eggplant cubes generously with salt and set them in a colander to drain. After 35 minutes, pat cubes dry with paper towels and set aside. Heat ¼ cup olive oil in a heavy skillet. Add celery and cook for 10 minutes over moderate heat, stirring often. Stir in onions and cook for an additional 8 to 10 minutes or until onions and celery are soft and lightly colored. With a slotted spoon transfer them to a bowl. Add remaining ¼ cup oil to skillet and sauté eggplant until it is lightly browned, stirring constantly. Return celery and onions to skillet. Add remaining ingredients. Bring to a boil and simmer uncovered for 15 minutes, stirring often. Flavor to taste with additional salt, pepper and vinegar. Refrigerate until ready to serve. Makes 8 cups, enough for 20 servings.

Best Liver Paté

¾ cup chopped scallions
1 clove garlic, minced
½ pound (2 sticks) butter
1 pound chicken livers
3 tablespoons cognac
⅛ teaspoon thyme

1½ teaspoons dry
   mustard
a dash each of nutmeg,
   cloves, mace
salt and pepper to taste

Sauté scallions and garlic in 3 tablespoons butter. Remove from pan. In same pan, sauté livers a few at a time in 2 tablespoons butter. Remove from sauté pan while slightly pink inside. Add cognac to pan. Ignite and pour over livers in an oven-proof dish. Put livers through fine-blade food grinder. Blend in the rest of the butter and spices. Add scallions and garlic and mix well. Season with salt and pepper to taste. Pour into mold. Chill until firm. To serve, unmold on platter or serve individual slices on bed of lettuce. Serves 12 to 15.

THE BRAMBLE INN
P.O. Box 159
Brewster, Massachusetts
02631
(617) 896-7644

MC/V/AE for meals only
Moderate

This Cape Cod inn is a haven for sports lovers, with the beach a 5-minute walk away, tennis courts adjacent, and golf and fishing nearby.

Oysters Perry Cabin

40 fresh-shucked oysters
  on the half-shell
10 slices bacon, quartered

1½ cups grated cheddar
  cheese

Leave oysters on the deep side of the shell, discarding other half of shell. Top each oyster with a bit of cheese and a piece of bacon. Broil for 5 minutes, or until bacon is crisp. Serve immediately (you can serve on a bed of rock salt to help retain heat). Serves 6 to 8.

THE INN AT
PERRY CABIN
St. Michaels, Maryland
21663
(301) 745-5178

MC/V/AE
Very expensive

Situated on the serene Miles River in the historic village of St. Michaels, this 6-room inn offers guests nearby sailing, antiquing and spectacular water fowl watching.

Stoddard-Cooper House Dip

1 pound cream cheese,
  softened
½ cup Major Grey
  chutney

½ cup toasted almonds
1 teaspoon curry
½ teaspoon mustard

Blend ingredients together and serve with crackers or celery. Serves 6 to 8.

STODDARD COOPER
HOUSE
19 West Perry Street
Savannah, Georgia
31401
(912) 233-6809

No credit cards
Expensive

This restored historic home with a single 2-bedroom suite offers the freedom of a private apartment with a beautiful hidden garden.

Tom's Treat

4 juice oranges, squeezed
four 5½-ounce cans
  apricot nectar
2 fresh limes, squeezed
½ cup juice drained from
  crushed pineapple

6 tablespoons canned
  cream of coconut
1 cup vodka or rum
  (optional)

Mix all juices and shake well. Great for breakfast. For an evening drink, add crushed ice and vodka or rum. Serves 8.

BARNARD-GOOD
HOUSE
238 Perry Street
Cape May, New Jersey
08204
(609) 884-5381

MC/V
Expensive

Good breakfast and warmth are the hallmarks of this resort-town inn, which also promises luxurious bathing in a copper tub.

THE BRADFORD INN

Liver Paté

1 stalk celery
3 sprigs parsley
6 whole peppercorns
1 quart water
1 pound chicken livers
½ medium onion
1 teaspoon salt

2 teaspoons dry mustard
½ teaspoon nutmeg
¼ teaspoon cloves
1 teaspoon Tabasco
½ clove garlic
1 cup (2 sticks) softened
    butter

Place celery, parsley and peppercorns in water and bring to a boil. Add livers and simmer for 15 minutes. Drain. Put livers and onions through food grinder, using finest blade. Blend in remaining ingredients. Pack in a mold. Wrap, seal, date and freeze. When ready to use, thaw in refrigerator. Makes 3 cups, serving 6 to 8.

BRADFORD INN
Main Street
Bradford, New Hampshire
03221
(603) 938-5309

No credit cards
Moderate

Owners of the Bradford Inn claim that there's "simply nothing to do" but relax, yet in the same breath offer 3 ski areas, lakes Sunapee and Massasecum, bicycles and rooms filled with interesting books.

THE INN AT MT. ASCUTNEY

Scotch Eggs

1 egg
1 pound sausage meat

bread crumbs
4 hard-boiled eggs, peeled

Preheat oven to 375°.

Mix egg and sausage meat. Divide mixture into 4 equal parts. Spread bread crumbs out on a plate. Mold sausage mixture around eggs, one at a time, and roll each one in the bread crumbs until it is spherical and well-coated. Place on a broiler rack in a jelly roll pan and cook for 45 minutes to one hour, or until sausage is well done. Serve hot, cold or warm with a little spicy mustard. Serves 12 as an appetizer or 4 as a main course with soup and salad.

THE INN AT
MT. ASCUTNEY
Brook Road
Brownsville, Vermont
05037
(802) 484-7725

MC/V
Moderate to expensive

A former farmhouse turned hilltop country inn, The Inn at Mt. Ascutney is graced with magnificent mountain views and a Cordon Bleu-trained chef.

THE VERMONT INN

Bloody Mary

2 cups V-8 Juice
2 ounces lemon and lime
   juice, mixed
2 teaspoons horseradish
4 dashes of Tabasco Sauce
4 dashes of Worcestershire
   Sauce

¼ teaspoon celery salt
¼ teaspoon salt
¼ teaspoon pepper
6 ounces vodka
4 wedges lime
4 stalks celery

Mix V-8 Juice with lemon-lime mix, horseradish, Tabasco and Worcestershire sauces, salt, pepper and vodka. Shake with cracked ice and strain into 4 large glasses over ice cubes. Garnish each with a wedge of lime and stalk of celery. Serves 4.

THE VERMONT INN
Route 41
Killington, Vermont
05751
(802) 773-9847

MC/V/AE
Expensive

The Vermont Inn is a favorite for winter vacations, with the Killington and Pico ski areas just minutes away. Rates are lower in summer, when the tennis courts and swimming pool are enticing attractions.

HOTEL LENADO

Hotel Lenado Hot Artichoke Dip

two 14-ounce cans
   artichoke hearts (not the
   marinated kind),
   drained and chopped
1 cup Parmesan cheese

1 cup shredded mozzarella
   cheese
1 cup mayonnaise
1 teaspoon salt
1 minced garlic clove

Preheat oven to 350°. Butter a soufflé dish or serving terrine.

Mix all ingredients thoroughly in a large bowl. Spoon mixture into prepared dish. Bake for 25 to 30 minutes. Serve hot with melba toast rounds or stoneground wheat crackers. Serves 10.

HOTEL LENADO
200 South Aspen Street
Aspen, Colorado 81611
(303) 925-6246
Reservations:
(303) 925-9000

MC/V/AE
Very expensive

This upscale inn—a new Aspen landmark—offers hot tub, sauna, swimming pool, bicycles, and tennis court.

Index